Insurgenc

C000116730

Insurgence is designed to help business leaders apply new methods to the most important business problem they face in the world today: namely, how to overcome their incumbent mentality to maintain relevance and discover new sources of growth. At the convergence of lean, business model innovation, agile, and design thinking, insurgence is a methodology and business philosophy that will help leaders in incumbent businesses rediscover how to operate like small and nimble insurgents whilst maintaining many of their incumbent advantages.

Incumbent businesses, often having enjoyed a long period of relative historical market stability, are increasingly unprepared for nimble insurgents coming on to the field of play and applying different assumptions and business models at speed and scale. These incumbent businesses find that the business models that fuelled their success are no longer robust to the change surrounding their business, and they are becoming increasingly obsolete, weighed down by a high degree of internal focus, inflexible internal controls, and an inability to innovate. Meanwhile, nimble insurgents strike at the heart of these weaknesses by formulating alternative core assumptions, building adaptive business models, and innovating in close proximity to customers and market needs.

This book enables business leaders to characterise the difference between incumbents and insurgents, develop new ways of thinking about how to compete in this age of accelerating change, and provide a new framework for strategy and innovation that helps leaders to discover the essence of insurgence for their businesses. It uses rich case studies that illustrate both successful and unsuccessful efforts to help leaders move from theory to action at speed and at scale.

Matthew Tice is the CEO of Insurgence Group, a management consulting firm dedicated to helping organisations to navigate and lead through disruptive change. Insurgence helps its clients at the nexus of strategy, innovation, and leadership to accelerate growth and build robust business models.

Insurgence

How Established Incumbents Can Operate Like Nimble Insurgents in Fast Changing and Volatile Markets

Matthew Tice

Routledge
Taylor & Francis Group

LONDON AND NEW YORK

First published 2020 by Routledge

2 Park Square, Milton Park, Abingdon, Oxon OX14 4RN
605 Third Avenue, New York, NY 10017

Routledge is an imprint of the Taylor & Francis Group, an informa business

First issued in paperback 2022

Copyright © 2020 Matthew Tice

The right of Matthew Tice to be identified as author of this work has been asserted by him in accordance with sections 77 and 78 of the Copyright, Designs and Patents Act 1988.

All rights reserved. No part of this book may be reprinted or reproduced or utilised in any form or by any electronic, mechanical, or other means, now known or hereafter invented, including photocopying and recording, or in any information storage or retrieval system, without permission in writing from the publishers.

Notice:
Product or corporate names may be trademarks or registered trademarks, and are used only for identification and explanation without intent to infringe.

Publisher's Note

The publisher has gone to great lengths to ensure the quality of this reprint but points out that some imperfections in the original copies may be apparent.

British Library Cataloguing-in-Publication Data
A catalogue record for this book is available from the British Library

Library of Congress Cataloging-in-Publication Data
A catalog record has been requested for this book

ISBN: 978-0-367-24440-8 (hbk)
ISBN: 978-1-03-233717-3 (pbk)
DOI: 10.4324/9780429282423

Typeset in Optima
by Deanta Global Publishing Services, Chennai, India

Contents

Contents

Foreword

My goal in writing this book is to help leaders to develop the capacity to transform their organisations in anticipation of disruption long before disruption knocks on their door. This topic is deeply personal to me having spent much of my career working with organisations of all types, often at the brink of extinction, to help reverse their fortunes in the face of disruption. In writing this book, I have become more and more convinced that disruption is a conscious or unconscious choice that leaders make for lack of will or preparation as change accelerates around the firm. Why would business leaders make this choice consciously? This is a complex question. No one wants to be disrupted but so often the choices made by leaders are limited by their perspective and deeply held assumptions. Just as a pilot, in a perfectly good aeroplane, can ignore the information in the cockpit in favour of their intuition only to fly into a mountain or the sea, so too can a leadership team, a board, or a family business owner miss the signs that are right in front of them and make fatal mistakes that can unravel a firm with a storied history in a very short period of time.

This book is intended for business leaders of all types and does not distinguish between industries, large and small, private and public, not-for-profit and government. These issues are universal. Business leaders, in my rather broad definition, include anyone with a stake in the business. This could be the CEO, the shop floor worker, middle manager, a customer, a board member, or a shareholder. Too often a firm's top leadership is expected to be omniscient and see change coming from every direction at once. This is unrealistic. They need help to gain perspective in times of change and the best leaders welcome additional perspective with open arms. I encourage leaders of all types and at all levels to help the organisation build awareness of what is happening outside and around the firm, challenge assumptions, and break down deeply embedded orthodoxy before it is too late.

Our company, Insurgence Group, exists to help companies across the economy to navigate the challenges described in this book. We founded the company to provide a resource for firms to help them navigate the increasing complexity in the world we live in. We work with both incumbents and insurgents in equal parts to initiate disruption and defend against it. As such, we spend every day in the trenches exploring the questions raised in this book and seek to find the elusive answers to these questions working closely with our clients, their customers, and sometimes even their competitors. It's a tremendous amount of fun. We freely admit that we don't have all of the answers and always try to prioritise asking great questions, seeking always to provide an alternative perspective to help our clients find new ways to see the world in which they operate.

Over the past 25 years, I have worked with dozens of organisations across most industries on six different continents on the challenges described in this book. The one thing I have learned is that there is always more to learn, and I invite feedback, case studies, and alternative perspectives from the reader to help expand my thinking on this topic for future projects and to improve the ideas outlined in this book. As such, I apologise in advance for any inaccuracies, omissions, or inconsistencies in what follows; these are as inevitable as they are unintentional.

Finally, I would like to acknowledge my thanks to Rondo Moses, my business partner in New York, for his patience, challenging ideas, and editing as this project developed. It would have been impossible to get this book finished without his calm encouragement.

Prologue

The one universal truth in business as we enter the middle part of the 21st century is that the pace of change is accelerating to such a degree that the foundations of the global economy and its participants are increasingly unstable for established players. Our research shows that more than 90% of business leaders believe that the markets in which they operate are increasingly unstable and subject to dramatic change over the next 5 years. We find that business leaders (including those in government and not-for-profit/for-purpose organisations) are grossly unprepared for this change on the one hand and are heavily reliant on the assumption of stability on the other.

This book explores the role of this instability and change on the decision-making processes of leaders as they formulate their strategies. In particular, we will explore the ability of incumbent businesses in established markets to adjust to accelerating change at scale relative to more nimble insurgent businesses seeking to disrupt the *status quo* as they challenge entrenched incumbents. Our work with leaders of businesses large and small over the past 25 years, in every sector of the economy and on six continents, leads us to conclude that the tools and methods available to leaders are fundamentally ill-suited for the task of navigating this change and, for the most part, are of best use only in situations where change is relatively slow, incremental, and predictable.

To frame the problem we seek to address in this book, we ask three fundamental questions that leaders must grapple with to maintain relevance:

Question 1: how stable is the environment surrounding your business?

We find that the leaders of most incumbent organisations, across almost all sectors, believe deeply that the environment surrounding their businesses is increasingly unstable, even precarious, and that "change is a given". Most leaders we work with acknowledge that change has always been a factor in business, but that the pace and the unpredictability of change today is profound. Yet, these leaders tend to operate their businesses, for the most part, on the assumption of stability without factoring in the consequences and speed of change. It should be noted that in highly stable environments (i.e., a low degree of change) incumbent players typically have the advantage and are able to operate in a relatively slow and incremental manner with little fear of disruption. The opposite is true in unstable environments. Instability breeds disruption and change and, therefore, favours the insurgent over the incumbent. If you believe that your business operates in a highly stable environment, congratulations; you can put this book down and keep doing what you are doing. If you are in the majority, however, it is essential that you are able to build a clear picture of how instability and change will affect your business.

Question 2: how robust is your business model to the change surrounding the business?

Before we frame this question, it is useful to clarify what we mean by a business model. Every organisation large and small has a business model. Put simply, a business model is a recipe for value creation (however value is defined). This recipe articulates the value proposition(s) that a firm takes to its customers, how the firm takes its products and services to market, how it configures its resources to deliver value to customers, and how it makes (and/or spends money). Business models are the skeleton of a business. In our experience, most business models are implicit, particularly in incumbent businesses. Often the business model of an organisation was created in past decades (or even past centuries) and as such the explicit visibility of the model to senior management is relatively low. When we ask senior managers (or even CEOs) to describe their business model, we are frequently surprised by how poorly they perform in articulating their business model and how that model creates value. In many cases, multiple generations of leadership (all tasked with perpetuation of the existing model) will even "forget" the business model and its founding assumptions (in practice, they are only vaguely aware of the business model). In incumbent firms, the business model doesn't typically get much attention or thought unless there is a major change that undermines the efficacy of the model. As often as not this change happens quite slowly then very quickly, leaving leaders unprepared and unable to respond. Robust business models are change-resilient and thus have a high tolerance for instability. In contrast to incumbents, insurgent businesses are typically highly aware of their business models, as meaningful differences in their models, as compared to incumbents, are required to compete and dislodge incumbents. Insurgents use market instability and change as their primary fuel to disrupt slow-moving incumbents by exploiting the incumbent's lack of awareness of its business model and its underpinning assumptions. We believe this question, i.e., "how robust is your business model to external change?" is one of the most important and fundamental questions of the age we live in for business leaders. If your business environment is unstable and your business model is not robust enough to handle this instability, your business is ripe for disruption and it is almost certainly inevitable.

Question 3: can established incumbents learn to operate like nimble insurgents?

The differences between incumbents and insurgents is a key theme of this book. Incumbents, having, historically, enjoyed a long period of relative market stability, are increasingly unprepared for nimble insurgents coming on to the playing field and applying different assumptions and business models at speed and scale. These incumbents are finding that the business models that fuelled their success are no longer robust to the change surrounding their businesses. These incumbents are thus becoming increasingly obsolete, weighed down by a high degree of internal focus, inflexible internal controls, and an inability to innovate. Meanwhile, nimble insurgents are striking at the heart of these weaknesses by formulating alternative core assumptions, building adaptive business models, and innovating in close proximity to customers and market needs. Unfortunately for incumbents, the tools and frameworks currently in use to build winning strategies and find innovative growth opportunities were designed for relatively stable and unchanging market conditions – these no longer serve them well or are ineffective in today's unstable conditions. Can incumbents discover the recipe for what makes insurgents succeed where they fail? This essence, "insurgence", defines the gap between incumbents and insurgents. In this book we will help business leaders to understand the difference between incumbents and insurgents, develop new ways of thinking about how to compete in this age of accelerating change, and provide a framework for strategy and innovation that helps leaders to discover the essence of insurgence for their businesses. We will use rich and familiar case studies that illustrate both successful and unsuccessful efforts to help leaders move from theory to action at speed and at scale.

The questions above are deeply personal to me. I have spent most of my career pursuing answers to these questions for clients around the world and across industries. I grew up in Rochester, New York, the home of Kodak. When I was in high school in the mid-1980s, Kodak reached its peak and yet was under threat, not from digital disruption but from Japanese and German competition that could offer the same or better products underpinned by more efficient production and, therefore, at a more competitive price. Kodak was the classic incumbent with nearly 100 years of rich heritage. My father and many of my friends and family worked at Kodak at the time. They were all aware of these challenges, and there was no question in any of their minds that Kodak could meet the threat posed by this competition. For the most part, this was true. The Japanese and German competition hardened Kodak against traditional competition and forced them to become more efficient. Kodak emerged stronger as a result, yet ironically less resilient. As this competition peaked, the introduction of digital imaging, a technology Kodak played a key role in inventing, became an even more significant threat. Watching from the outside and listening to people involved in the business, it became clear that Kodak was unable to adapt to the change. Year after year reductions in workforce were announced and one friend or family member after another was made redundant until finally Kodak emerged as a shell of its former self, another of the great brands of the world relegated to obscurity. My father bowed out relatively early in the fight, taking early retirement in the late 1990s.

How could a well-funded and well-established incumbent get it so wrong? Were they not paying attention? Were they unaware of the changes coming their way? My hypothesis is that Kodak was unable to answer the questions we have outlined above. When Fuji Film came onto the scene in the 1980s, whilst this represented a change, certainly a challenge to the leading incumbent, the market was still operating by a set of rules and assumptions largely defined by Kodak. As digital imaging evolved, Kodak made the fatal assumption that the underlying fabric of the market for film was largely stable. Kodak assumed that the business model that carried it successfully for nearly a century would be sufficient to take them forward into the next century. Finally, they assumed that they could rewrite the new rules of competition in digital imaging to their advantage. In this case, unfortunately for Kodak, the incumbent was not able to compete with the insurgents.

It turns out that this pattern repeats in almost every case of disruption we have come across and is not industry- or sector-dependant. The pattern is the same in business to business (B2B) and business to consumer (B2C) cases as well as for not-for-profits. Kodak had 25 years to adjust to the disruption. What is increasingly clear is that 25 years was a luxury. For many firms, the time from awareness of a disruptive threat to death can be as short as 12–18 months. Our purpose in writing this book is to help leaders reframe their thinking *and* learn how to apply the essence of "insurgence" to their business to avoid and/or initiate disruption successfully.

1 The age of insurgence

When we speak with CEOs of businesses of all sizes, they generally fall into two groups, those that play offence and those that play defence. It is much easier to play defence as a large and complex incumbent business than it is to play offence. The numbers alone demonstrate the reasons for this. If you are the leader of a business or business unit operating with a market share of more than 50% (not necessarily a definition of incumbent), the marginal effort required to get to 51% market share is significantly more difficult than the marginal effort to defend the existing 50% (all things being equal). As businesses mature, it is inevitable that the pendulum shifts from offence to defence. A business that is focused on defending its position is highly vulnerable to disruption in unstable markets. A defensive posture creates a set of behaviours in the firm that makes rapid action all but impossible. The default mindset of the incumbent is defensive precisely because it is easier in the short term to play defence than offence (and because the penalties for losing can be much harsher than the rewards for winning). The more mature an industry and the more established the incumbent firm is, the truer this becomes. With market share gains and losses often represented in basis points, incumbents are highly aware that it can take years to recover from even the smallest stumble. This dynamic creates an environment that significantly reduces the scope of innovation in the business and starves the business of resources to pursue new opportunities (with the exception of M&A) for fear of cannibalisation of the existing business (after all, why would the film team at Kodak with products generating, say, 85% gross margins give up any market share to the digital team with products that have uncertain futures, negligible gross margins, and limited scale?).

Insurgents are unburdened by many of the constraints of the incumbent. Insurgents are programmed to play *only* offence after all, as they don't typically have anything to defend, instead focusing on growth. Their opportunities usually, though not always, come at the expense of an incumbent (though the incumbent may not be in the same industry). Insurgents don't worry about cannibalisation of existing products and services and are more than happy to replace low performers with higher-performing products. The risk profile of insurgents is different. Insurgents have to grow and scale to materially threaten incumbents. The metrics that they pursue to achieve this are fundamentally different than those operated by the incumbent (e.g., time to minimum viable product, acquisition rate of new customers, and cash burn). As such the insurgent has far fewer constraints, at least in the scope of their thinking (but typically far fewer material resources), than the typical incumbent.

There have always been and will always be incumbents and insurgents. What is different in the current age is the pace at which insurgents are challenging and disrupting incumbents and the speed at which the insurgents are able to grow to scale (thus becoming the next generation of incumbents). Another difference is the amount of funding available to insurgents and, perhaps, the metrics that insurgents are judged by in the market as many insurgents are judged on their growth not on their profitability in the early stages (sometimes for a decade or more). An additional note is that the power of both incumbents and insurgents is growing. How is this possible? Well-funded insurgents, on the one hand, are challenging almost every market. At the same time, established market-leading incumbents are increasing their power in many sectors of the economy (*The Economist*, 2018). The firms in the middle, in between these two poles, are especially vulnerable. These firms must discover and implement the key ingredients of the insurgent to successfully adapt to change in their markets.

In our work with clients and on the speaking circuit, there is a consistent pushback about the term "disruption". While this is not a book about disruption *per se*, a key thesis of the book is that disruption is both real and inevitable. Usually, we hear people say, "disruption has always been there, there is nothing new about disruption" or "disruption is a fad". On the first point, we agree. Disruption has always existed; from horses to railroads to cars, from whale oil to electricity, from film to digital, one paradigm inevitably gives way to another. That said, the term "disruption" is beginning to create a bit of a "gag factor" for many people now as it has become so pervasive in business. Unfortunately for many, and fortunately for some, disruption is not a fad. Just ask Hillary Clinton. She will probably tell you that disruption is not only real but has leaked out from business into politics and into other parts of the world we live in (parenting comes to mind).

As a thought exercise, I was interested in the earliest possible disruption case I could find that would best illustrate, in particular, the difference between the incumbent and the insurgent. Looking back *thousands* of years, I landed on an example (Matthews, 2019) that I think tells a very interesting story about the disruption dynamic.

The backdrop to the Battle of Carrhae is Rome in the late republic on one side and the Parthian empire on the other. During this time, power in Rome was split three ways by the "First Triumvirate" represented by Julius Caesar, Marcus Crassus, and Gnaeus Pompey. At that time, Pompey the Great was the "old salt" military commander with fame as the greatest Roman general of his age; concurrently, Julius Caesar was ascendant and earning laurels for his success in his Gaul campaigns and Marcus Crassus was the richest man in Rome and reportedly one of the richest people in all of history but lacking in military glory the chief political currency of the age. Unfortunately, success on the battlefield and conquest counted for more than money in league tables of the time and Marcus Crassus, in an attempt to prove himself worthy of Caesar and Pompey, embarked on a campaign to invade Parthia to enhance his stature and earn glory on the battlefield. At that time Rome and Parthia were not at war. It is unknown what the invasion pretext was that Crassus used to justify the invasion, but it is well known that Crassus pursued the invasion to enhance his own political status. In all, Crassus employed some seven legions of about 35,000 heavy infantry, an additional 4,000 light infantry, and approximately 4,000 combined horse cavalry including 1,000 cavalry sourced from Gaul by his son Publius, in all a formidable force (Wasson, 2019).

Parthia at that time represented an empire to the East of Rome in ancient Mesopotamia (a significant part of modern Iran). The Parthian response to the Roman invasion was significantly more modest employing approximately 9,000 horse archers and 1,000 cataphracts (heavily armoured cavalry), in all about one-quarter the size of the Roman force. The Parthian force was led by Spahbed Surena (General Surena).

The following exhibits describe the two adversaries in the battle. Exhibit 1 shows a cut-out image of the Roman infantry. It is worth taking a moment to describe what is shown in the exhibit in detail. The first impression of the Roman soldier is professionalism. The livery and orderly formation speaks to a highly professional and well-disciplined army. The soldiers are well armed and heavily armoured, and their leadership is in the background directing the action of the soldiers. This speaks to a highly regimented command structure.

Exhibit 1 Roman infantry.

It is also worth noting that the soldiers are on foot, carrying a heavy load (shield, sword, spear, armour, provisions, etc.). The background suggests that the battle is being fought in the desert. It is hard to imagine that the soldiers, used to fighting in the temperate climes surrounding the Mediterranean Sea, would not have been very hot and uncomfortable in the desert, let alone the battle. It was usual for the Roman infantry to deploy with infantry at the centre and the cavalry at the flanks; however, it is known that as Crassus deployed for battle, the legions deployed in a hollow square to counteract the Parthian cavalry. In this formation and with this amount of gear, the Roman army lacked mobility and ability to strike at any distance. While the Roman army was numerically superior in total, the Parthian cavalry significantly outnumbered the Roman cavalry.

The Parthians, shown in Exhibit 2, can be seen as a highly mobile force of horse archers and cataphracts (cataphracts not pictured). The differences are stark by comparison. The Parthians appear comfortable in livery well suited to the desert environment (note the lack of standardisation of the livery). As horse archers, the Parthian force is highly mobile and able to strike at a significant distance. Cataphracts are armoured heavy horse cavalry designed to punch through set formations of infantry (not shown). It also appears that the Parthian force is more opportunistic and less reliant on command and control. All of these factors represent significant differences relative to the Roman model.

Exhibit 2 Parthian horse archers. Illustration by Angus McBride in Karasulas, A, (2019) *Mounted Archers of the Steppe 600 BC–AD 1300*. Osprey Publishing, Oxford.

As the battle unfolded, the Romans, led by Crassus, attacked the Parthians first. The Parthians responded by pouring arrows into the Roman force at a distance, inflicting damage without significant risk to their own force. Each time the Romans attacked, the Parthians fled to safety and continued to harass the Romans with arrows at a safe distance. Eventually, the Romans realised that the Parthians would whittle them down over time if they were not able to force a decisive ground engagement. Once the battle was committed, the opportunity for the Romans to retreat was limited as their exposure to the missiles in retreat would have been fatal. As such, the Roman strategy for the battle was to form a square in *testudo* (turtle) formation and take the fire until the Parthians exhausted their arrows.

Meanwhile, the Parthians realised that in spite of a numerically inferior force, they could attack the Romans with impunity as long as their arrows held out. To facilitate this, the Parthians arranged for camel trains to resupply their arrows to ensure that they would have sufficient supply for the battle. Once the Romans formed Testudo as shown in Exhibit 1, the Parthians employed their cataphracts to disrupt the Roman square and open up juicy targets for the horse archers.

The Romans, having realised that the Parthians were resupplying their archers via camel train, employed their own cavalry in an attempt to disrupt the Parthian supply lines. This force was led by Publius Crassus, the son of Marcus Crassus. Unfortunately, as it turned out, the Roman cavalry, designed for close infantry support and not for battle against horse archers, proved as unable to compete against the Parthian horse archers as their infantry was and was defeated in detail. Publius committed suicide and the remainder of his cavalry force was killed or captured.

Eventually, the Parthians cut the Roman force to pieces with combined cataphract and horse archer attacks. The Romans were defeated, and Marcus Crassus was killed in the battle. The rout was comprehensive and a significant embarrassment to the "invincible" Roman army.

How is it that a numerically inferior force could disrupt and defeat a superior and well-disciplined force and why would we bother using this example to illustrate the roles of incumbents and insurgents as an analogy for disruption?

This is one of my favourite examples of disruption for many reasons (not least of which that it is not digital in nature). The characteristics of this battle are very applicable to the business context when one takes a closer look. Starting with the Romans, what we see is as follows:

1. What are the Romans solving for? The basis for the battle itself was the fame and glory of Marcus Crassus. This is hardly a compelling and motivating proposition as compared to the Parthians who were defending their homes from the aggressors. As such, Marcus Crassus incompetently read the situation and made numerous mistakes based on his own inflated sense of his command ability and his innate belief in the "invincibility" of the Roman war machine.

2. The Roman "business model", while well suited for the Mediterranean context, was grossly inadequate for the Parthian context (the desert). The Romans fatally assumed that their superiority in numbers (mistake 1) and in war fighting (mistake 2) made them unbeatable. This outlines the importance of context. As the Romans entered a new context (the environment was unfamiliar and therefore unstable) that they were not familiar with, their key war-fighting assumptions (climate, tactics, etc.) no longer applied as they encountered an adversary that was both better adapted to the context (the Parthian desert) and able to exploit every single weakness of the Roman force, including strategy and tactics as well as important details such as the comfort and mobility of the soldiers in the desert (the workforce).

3. The Romans assumed that the Parthians would fight the battle on their terms and under their rules – the Parthians did not take the bait. As a smaller force, they had no choice but to fight the battle in a completely different way (in the modern lingo, asymmetrically). The idea that the Parthians would not fight an honourable "set piece" infantry engagement never occurred to the Romans.

The Parthians (let's call them the insurgents in this example, though a purist might argue that the Romans were invading) were able to exploit each and every flawed assumption that the Romans brought to the battle. The Romans (the incumbent force in this example) were plagued by a failure to understand the differences in context and the resulting breakdown of the assumptions that they brought to the engagement. These factors, coupled with the arrogance and hubris of the Roman leadership, brought them to disaster. As we will show later in the book, this pattern is very common to incumbents who are used to winning in a particular context. As the conditions surrounding the organisation (in this case, the desert, the competition, and the reasons for fighting) change, the business often fails to recognise these changes and leaves itself wide open for disruption.

As we fast forward 2,000 years, these lessons are highly relevant to businesses in the modern context. Many of the ingredients of disruption described above still apply today. In our experience the application of a different model, operating under different rules and assumptions, brought forward by the insurgent to undermine the established incumbent is a pattern that repeats over and over in the majority of cases of disruption. Why then is it so difficult for us to take these lessons to heart (in the case of incumbents) and apply them to our businesses?

2016 USA election

In the leadup to the 2016 USA presidential election, Mrs. Hillary Clinton was all but convinced that her bid to win the election was a given. Mrs. Clinton ran a very professional campaign and performed well in the polls, on the fundraising circuit, and in the debates. Smart money had Mrs. Clinton winning the election by a small but comfortable margin. Mrs. Clinton was the establishment (incumbent) candidate, part of a modern "dynasty" that started with her husband's, Bill Clinton, two successful terms as president and continued through her term in the United States Senate and as the secretary of state in the Obama administration. More than almost anyone in politics at that time, Mrs. Clinton had an almost insurmountable incumbent advantage.

Yet Mrs. Clinton was not successful. The insurgent, Donald Trump, was able to exploit almost every single weakness that Mrs. Clinton brought to the campaign. Mr. Trump and his campaign team knew all too well that they were unable to, using the Roman analogy, fight an open battle against the Clinton machine. To win, he had to play a different game, use a different set of rules, and undermine each aspect of the Clinton election machine. Mrs. Clinton had many advantages, Mr. Trump had one. The key advantage that Mr. Trump brought to the table was not a superior message (though his message was resonant) but a deep understanding of how Mrs. Clinton would respond, as the incumbent, to his insurgent campaign. Just as the Parthians knew that the Romans would deploy in a hollow square to defend against horse archers, Mr. Trump was able to predict and disrupt the Clinton campaign at every turn. It appears that Mrs. Clinton was placing greater emphasis on winning the popular vote (which she won) having neglected a couple of key rust belt states in her campaign, whilst Mr. Trump was solving for winning the electoral college (which he won). His approach in every aspect of the campaign was different. While Mrs. Clinton took the high road, he took the low road; he undermined her credibility in the popular media, abusing Mrs. Clinton about her use of personal accounts for government emails, he controlled the popular press, and the list goes on *ad infinitum*.

Above all, Mr. Trump was incredibly close to his base (his customers) and highly in tune with their needs and frustrations. Mrs. Clinton was aloof to the "unwashed masses" and even referred to some of them as "deplorables". She was distant from the people casting the votes. Mr. Trump was in the trenches everyday speaking directly to the needs of his "customers" and successfully peeling off thousands of voters who otherwise would have voted for Mrs. Clinton. This degree of proximity to the voter/customer is a key characteristic of the insurgent. As incumbents become less and less attuned to the needs of their customers and more and more internally focused, insurgents are often able to undermine the incumbent's position with their customers just as Mr. Trump did in the 2016 election.

The same patterns apply in business. Disruption in business, while at times driven by a fundamentally new product or technology, most often starts with an unstable context, a lazy or inward-looking incumbent (or many as the case may be) and an insurgent that is both willing and able to play by a different set of rules (or even laws) than the incumbent. Uber, perhaps the most overused example of disruption in modern literature, is nevertheless a great example of this dynamic.

How could an upstart company like Uber (and Lyft, Grab, etc.) so profoundly challenge the established taxi industry so quickly? Let's first explore the dynamics of the incumbent. Prior to Uber, the taxi industry worldwide, with few exceptions, had very similar characteristics. The industry was typically set up as a quasi-regulated monopoly whereby the government (different countries have different regimes for managing taxi licences) would offer or auction taxi licences (the right to operate taxis) at a level where demand exceeded supply, i.e., more demand for taxi rides than supply of available taxis. As a result, the revenue from licences for taxis would often approach millions of dollars (of revenue to the state) in many cases. In practice this means that, in most jurisdictions, the majority of taxi licences are tightly held by a few players or syndicates. Independent taxis, while available, would have to work so hard to pay back the financing on the licenses, often to the point of poverty, that the incentives to own a single licence were very limited and, therefore, favoured corporate or syndicate ownership of the licenses. In addition, the prices offered to taxi consumers are set by the state (flag fall plus rate per mile or minute), putting a ceiling on the return a taxi could generate.

To keep costs down and to ensure return on capital and profitability, the licence holders would typically employ low-wage and inexperienced drivers (London and Singapore being notable exceptions in my experience). As such, the customer experience could be described as poor. In my own experience, I have encountered taxis that were poorly maintained, half full of vomit from the night before, and often driven by people who were unfamiliar with both the geography and the language in the area of operation. For decades, this "unholy alliance" between licence holder and local governments perpetuated a model that created an incredibly poor experience for consumers. Along came Uber (and others).

Uber, on one level, is not very different from a taxi. The end result of moving from A to B for a consumer, in a car, is still largely the same. Yet the business models behind the consumer transaction are very different. Like Mr. Trump, Uber discovered an arrogant, perhaps lazy incumbent operating by a defined set of rules in a fast changing and unstable market. In times past, consumers were willing to accept a poor experience offered by an inferior supplier (in this case, the taxi) mainly because there were no other options. But this is no longer the case in general as consumer empowerment is now quite pervasive. As such, consumers were "ready" for the change when Uber came on the scene. Also, changes in technology, particularly the ubiquity of smartphones and the apps that go with them, created an unstable environment for taxi companies even though they were, for the most part, unaware of this instability or at least unwilling to confront it given their established position in the market.

Uber upturned almost every single assumption held by the incumbent taxi industry. Table 1 presents a short and non-exhaustive list.

When you look at the differences described in Table 1, it becomes clear that behind the transportation from point A to point B, almost *everything* is different. This includes, notably, the Uber position that the regulated monopoly was fundamentally unfair to consumers and that the legislation surrounding the incumbent taxi industry would not stand up to challenge (while this has not proven to be universally true, Uber has forced many local governments worldwide to change legislation to allow them to operate in competition with taxis).

In all of these cases, the insurgent was able to challenge the underlying assumptions of the incumbent by offering up an alternative model that fundamentally altered the competitive landscape based on the exploitation of a change in context (terrain, consumer behaviour, technology, etc.). These factors are at the core of disruption.

Table 1 Taxi vs. Uber Business Model

Assumption	Taxi	Uber
Taxi license	Purchase at auction. Hold and trade	No licence
Customer experience	Take what you get	Frictionless payment, friendly drivers, multisided ratings
Fare	Regulated	Set by the market – surge pricing when busy
Dispatch	Centralised and manual	Decentralised and technology-enabled
Fleet	Owned and leased	Provided mostly by drivers using their own vehicles
Workforce	Low-wage labour – indentured servants	Full- and part-time gigs – drivers employing spare time mostly on their own terms
Maintenance	Maintenance facility in centralised pooling location	Set standards for vehicles owned by drivers
Safety	Physical barrier between consumer and driver	Transparency of location and driver ratings

References

Karasulas, A, 2004, *Mounted Archers of the Steppe 600 BC–AD 1300*. Osprey Publishing, Oxford.

Matthews, R, 2019, The Battle of Carrhae 53 BC, *Encyclopaedia Britannica*, https://britannica.com/event/Battle-of-Carrhae.

The Economist, 2018, Schumpeter: 2018 will be the year that big, incumbent companies take on big tech, https://economist.com/business2018/01/03/2018-will-be-the-year-that-big-incumbent-companies-take-on-big-tech.

Wasson, D, 2019, Battle of Carrhae, 53 BC, *Ancient History Encyclopedia*, https://ancient.eu/article/1406/battle-of-carrhae-53-bce.

2 Checkers and chess

In our work, we are fortunate to interact with dozens of companies each year around the world and speak with hundreds of CEOs and senior executives at various functions, conferences, roundtables, and speaking engagements. As such, we are exposed to countless strategies and "strategic plans" each year with clients and organisations seeking advice on how to better perform, initiate, or defend against disruption, execute strategies, etc. While some of the companies are start-ups or insurgents, many are incumbents in well-established industries. One question which we like to explore as we look at these strategies and plans is "what is strategy?"

The most common answers to the question can be listed below, an amalgamation of the top answers from the hundreds of CEOs we ask this question each year. Here are the top five:

1. A roadmap – how to get from point A to point B
2. A vision and a set of goals to achieve them
3. "The how"
4. A plan of action
5. What you are going to do and what you are not going to do

This is the standard frame for strategy in our experience. An immediate observation from the list above is that all of these points are made from the *internal* point of view of the company or firm. What I mean by this is that the perspective of the above is basically "what we want as a firm and how we are going to get it". Having reviewed dozens of strategies and plans in the past year and hundreds more over the past 25 years, 90% of the strategies we see follow the above pattern, i.e., are company centric. OK, so what?

Let's start with a simple thought experiment to illustrate the point. If I asked you to imagine a chessboard with blue pieces on one side and red pieces on the other, I am sure that the image would come to mind handily. As chess is often used as an analogy for strategy, we will use it here to demonstrate what strategy is and the flaws in how companies typically think about strategy.

Imagine a chess game between two players in an established market, a duopoly. Let's use Coca-Cola and Pepsi to illustrate the game. In our example, Pepsi will be represented by the blue player and Coca-Cola will be represented the red player. Next, imagine each time a player moves a piece that this represents a move in the marketplace. Let's begin.

Let's assume that the leadership of both organisations have spent some time upfront determining how they will play the game, in other words, what they are *solving for*. Since it is not a given that they are solving for the same thing, it is useful to mention up front that Pepsi might be solving for short-term profits, and Coca-Cola might be solving for market share. The first move goes to Pepsi. They move a bishop (the game is already underway after all) and this represents the introduction of a new high-margin probiotic product to market. What happens next? Coca-Cola needs to respond (or not) by evaluating the new product and deciding how to counter the move, perhaps introducing another product, a copycat product, or making some other move altogether. Coca-Cola decides to put more emphasis on an existing product and not enter the probiotic market. Pepsi is up again, this time a move of the queen representing entering a new market (Namibia, for example). Again, Coca-Cola is given a turn and has to decide to respond or to make another move altogether. In this next move, Coca-Cola, already represented in the market Pepsi chose to enter, decides to lower prices in that market to prevent Pepsi from gaining market share. And so, the game goes on back and forth.

Let us now look at what is happening. Each business in this simple example is positioning relative to the other. Whilst each company has made some decisions upfront about what they are solving for in the game, once these decisions are made, the game is all about move/countermove to gain advantage relative to the competition. Unfortunately, as the chessboard is only two-dimensional, we are missing an important stakeholder, the consumer. The consumer gets a vote each time the company makes a move on the board. Will the consumer respond to Pepsi's probiotic product? Will the consumer buy more product from Coca-Cola following their price drop?

The point is that strategy is *positional*. The positioning of Coca-Cola vs. Pepsi (and the consumer) is the heartland of strategy. Still, the analogy is insufficient. Surrounding Coca-Cola and Pepsi is an environmental context. This context, as mentioned above, may be stable or changing rapidly. Changes in the context (new technology, consumer behaviour, changes in regulation, corn syrup commodity prices, etc.) all inevitably factor into the decisions the players make in the game of competition. The more the context changes, the harder the game is to play (imagine someone shaking up the board whilst you are trying to move your pieces). Finally, what drops out are options or choices available to the players (i.e., I can move my knight but not my rook because of where they are positioned on the board). Exhibit 3 illustrates the "holy trinity of strategy". The positioning of the company relative to the competition and the customer (or consumer) in a given environment (changing context) will deliver certain choices available to each player in the market.

Most "strategies" do not follow this pattern. Most "strategies" are what we would describe as "inside-out" planning, not strategy. In other words, these "strategies" skip the strategy part and go straight for the plan. This usually starts with a vision statement and then follows with goals/objectives, a budget, and a commitment to deliver to some target. Operating managers are then asked to deploy resources accordingly. In some cases, the plans are very sophisticated, but the strategies are non-existent, that is to say that the context, competition, and the customer barely factor into the planning, if at all. In a world where none of these factors are changing and all of the variables are well known (who is the competition? How will customers behave? etc.), i.e., a stable market, this approach, while insufficient, is better than nothing. Exhibit 3 below describes

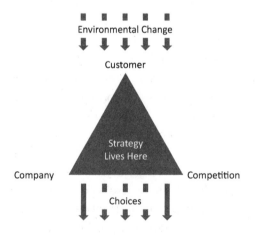

Exhibit 3 Holy trinity of strategy.

this dynamic. The inside-out strategist creates detailed plans based only on what the company wants, often, if not always, "more" (more revenue, more profit, more products, etc.). This type of planning goes in only one direction, up. These "strategies" are *internally focused* projections of the existing business into the market. In practice, these are not strategies at all, but plans, an important distinction. Sound familiar? This is probably how your company develops its "strategy".

As I share the chess analogy, I can now reveal that this is a very bad analogy for many reasons. The business world has *n* competitors and *n* customers after all, and a chessboard has just two competitors on a very restricted playing field. Chess is a zero-sum game, business is not. As mentioned above, the customer is not represented on the board. Still, this analogy serves well enough for companies operating in a stable environmental context if you use your imagination. Even so, most companies, even in a stable context, do not rigorously evaluate the interplay between context, competition, and customers but rather focus on vision/objectives/targets.

The real breakdown of the chess analogy is that most companies (more than 90%) do not view their context as stable. A disruptive world does not look at all like a chess game. Implicit in the game of chess is a set of rules that all players are bound by. As such, the moves available to a player, while expansive, are limited by the board, the piece (a bishop may only move diagonally, for example), and their positioning on the board. These rules are fundamental and immutable in the game. Two incumbents that have been playing "chess" for a long time eventually take the established rules as a given. The rules themselves are seldom challenged, better the "devil you know" perhaps. The assumptions about how the competition (and the consumer) might behave are also not typically challenged. The world of the incumbent strategist can be often described as playing an inside-out game of chess moving pieces in complete ignorance of how the other player(s) move their pieces. This may sound harsh, but it is true much more often than not.

Insurgents don't play chess. Insurgents watch incumbents playing chess and then play Go, or Checkers, or Backgammon. You see the point, a *different game* altogether. All the rules and assumptions underpinning how an incumbent player will play the game become critical weaknesses to be exploited by insurgents. It is unusual for an incumbent to become thoroughly disrupted by another chess player playing the same game, at least in the short to middle term, unless there is a measure of incompetence at work. For example, Nokia (consumer mobile phones) was not disrupted by Ericsson but by Apple with the iPhone/iTunes/App ecosystem. Insurgents are prepared to overturn every single rule and assumption that the incumbent takes for granted, many of which are partly or even entirely invisible to the incumbent.

If you are reading this, chances are you are an incumbent and are very unprepared for a change in the game. First, you are programmed to look inside the business and have a plan to get what you want, not a strategy – you live in your own bubble. The good news is that this can be fixed. The bad news is once it's fixed, you are still highly vulnerable to being disrupted by an insurgent if you are in the majority (unstable market context, a business model that is not robust to change, and an inside-out frame of reference).

The tools and methods available to organisations when it comes to strategy and planning are not well-suited for unstable market contexts. The majority of the methods employed in strategy design (e.g., SWOT, PESTEL, etc.) are no longer sufficient, if they ever were. Most of these tools assume at their core that the fundamental fabric (industry business models and key assumptions) underpinning the business context is fixed (i.e., the rules of the game). Two-dimensional "paint by numbers" methodologies create lazy thinking, and lazy thinking leads to vulnerable companies.

Strategy is fundamentally an "outside-in" game and exists only in the context of external forces acting on the firm (competitors, customers, trends, etc.). To be successful at creating strategy, firms must train their managers to transcend the planning paradigm and reorient their thinking to look at the firm objectively from the point of view of the market, including players and customers outside of the usual frame of reference. While difficult, this is important, especially as previously well-defined industries blend together and cross traditional boundaries. Your future competition is lurking in the shadows, invisible to you if you do not open up your perspective. Nokia did not see Apple, a computer company, as a credible threat until it was too late. Apple did not define themselves as a phone handset company at that time but as a platform, bringing together the phone, the development community, and the consumer to create something fundamentally different than what existed previously. This required a blending of industries and capabilities. Equally, the trends that might impact your business in the future are also possibly invisible to you owing to your limited perspective. Your future competitors can turn insight into these trends into opportunities at your expense. Certainly, having a strategy is important and executing that strategy through a well-resourced plan is as, if not more, important. Chances are you are doing too much of the latter and not enough of the former. Food for thought.

Key takeaways:

1. Strategy is not a plan – you probably have a plan and not a strategy
2. Most plans go in one direction – up
3. Strategy is an outside-in game, not an inside-out game; play accordingly
4. A strategy built for a stable environmental context is not sufficient to navigate unstable conditions
5. Insurgents don't play by the same rules as incumbents; they play a different game with different assumptions
6. Incumbents are typically unaware of the foundational assumptions underpinning their business models
7. The tools you are using are (probably) not well-suited to help you navigate or initiate disruption

3 | Defining insurgence

What if an incumbent, particularly a large and complex organisation, could operate at scale like an insurgent? What would the main ingredients of the insurgent be and how could these be applied to the incumbent? Is incumbent status an inevitable consequence of maturity? We will dedicate the remainder of the book to exploring these themes.

According to *Merriam Webster Dictionary* (2019), insurgence can be defined as "the act or action of being insurgent".

An insurgent, as you will have guessed, is akin to a rebel or a disruptor seeking to displace the established order in a way that favours their view of the world at the expense of the existing prevailing view. In biology, an insurgent can be seen as an invasive species; in politics, a rebel group or person seeking to upset the existing order; and in business, a new competitor seeking to reframe how value is created against established players, i.e., incumbents.

Our definition of insurgence is a bit broader and could be articulated as the "defining characteristics, mindset and behaviours of an insurgent". We seek to understand these characteristics and create a general set of principles that define the insurgent mindset such that would-be insurgents and incumbents alike can understand and apply "insurgence" as a capability to better position themselves in the marketplace. In this application, firms will hopefully be better prepared for disruption and more resilient in the future as they formulate and execute their strategies.

The following case study is based loosely on a real business; however, the names, facts, and locations are entirely fictional to protect the privacy of the founders of the business.

Caly's Frozen Yogurt Co, Inc.

I first came across Caly's more than 20 years ago, a few years after its founding in Ann Arbor, Michigan. The business was established in 1994 by Carl and Ally Andrews (hence the name Caly's) as a retail frozen yogurt business. I first met Ally at the University of Michigan in the late 1980s. The business, typical of many frozen yogurt businesses of the time, was initially a relatively simple business in a crowded market. Located in a large university town, the business catered to students and local residents alike. Both Carl and Ally attended business school to learn how to grow and run their business. Ally in particular can be best described as an entrepreneur, always willing to try new things and innovate. Carl is the "numbers guy" and is very astute at managing operations.

Carl attended business school first, followed by Ally two years later. In their strategy course at business school, they learned the basic structure of strategic planning and applied this thinking to develop a vision statement for their business. Like all vision statements (disclaimer, I am not a fan of vision statements), theirs read something like "to be the #1 yogurt and ice cream retailer in the Greater Ann Arbor area and to enable access to Caly's within a 5-minute walk anywhere on campus". At the time of their founding, this was a particularly aggressive and seemingly impossible task given the competition, a fragmented array of "mom and pop" purveyors spread across the town with no clear leader in the market. To facilitate their planning, they created a map of the town and built a model to illustrate the locations of all of their competition and, at the time, the location of their first shop relative to the competition. They worked out that the market had room for ten additional shops (various footprints and assuming the closure of some of the existing shops in the market) and that, if strategically located, these shops would allow them to achieve their vision on both counts (market dominance and market access).

Having defined where the business would operate and broadly how best to position the business relative to their then competition, Ally and Carl moved on to defining a value proposition that would be sufficiently differentiated from the competition and that would engage their target market, the university student. The model that they landed on was way ahead of its time, one of the first "experience" restaurants. They worked out that studying was hungry work and that students often would come into the store in small groups to study, eat yogurt and other sundry items, and relax. Being very aware of this theme, Ally and Carl created a theme that was all about "a safe place to study, eat ice cream and relax". In effect, Ally and Carl were giving the students an alternative to studying in the library (no food allowed) and focusing on campus safety, particularly in late evening hours by providing access to the campus security network, bright outdoor lighting, etc. As Wi-Fi became available, Caly's was one of the first businesses to offer free Wi-Fi and they made power outlets available near the tables for students to plug in laptops and, eventually, other devices such as phones and tablets.

Ally, an amateur artist, has a keen eye for design and developed a funky and fun on-trend design concept for the restaurants. Students and locals alike loved it. Customers flocked to the store and before long Ally and Carl were on their way to opening up a new restaurant at a pace of about one every 12–18 months. Very quickly the business became an icon of the town and Ally and Carl found themselves heavily involved in the local business community as participants in the community and as mentors. To keep things fresh as the business grew, Ally and Carl would update the look and feel of their restaurants on a cycle of about every three years, freshening up the colour schemes, technology, and menu to maintain relevance. To facilitate this, they went on annual study tours to look at how other, similar businesses were run around the country and to draw inspiration from these businesses that could be applied back home. Relatively quickly, they discovered that there wasn't much to learn from benchmarking their peers and, instead, decided to look at tea houses in places like New York City and San Francisco as well as paint shops. The tea houses proved valuable as a source of inspiration for on-trend flavours and decor (these also being source markets for many students), and the paint shops were helpful to give inspiration for the colour palette for both the decor and the product. For example, jasmine tea and honey ice cream was a particularly popular flavour. Yogurt and ice cream, being very tactile products, lend themselves very well to colourful design. Creating a unified look and feel to the product and the environment is a key part of the Caly's experience.

As the business developed over 20 years, Carl and Ally began to achieve their goals through hard work and by paying careful attention to product development, enhancing the restaurant experience, and listening to their customers. By 2012, they opened their 11th restaurant achieving the original milestone set forth in their vision statement. By that time, the business was turning over about $1 million per restaurant *per annum* ($11 million in total) and had a roster of about 250 employees working three shifts at all their restaurants. Market leadership followed their rise and eventually Caly's crowded out their competition achieving almost 80% market share in the category (retail frozen yogurt, ice cream, and, eventually, gelato). Ally and Carl made a deliberate decision not to sell the business or to grow the business out beyond the borders of the city. Their goal was eventually to have their children run the business after they retired.

As the business became more successful, it also became a local institution. Every university town has its famous restaurants and Ann Arbor is no exception. Somehow, these businesses become "must visit" places for students and alumni alike in spite of the typical four-year turnover of the student population. Caly's rapidly became one of these few places where everyone goes and comes back to.

In 2007, the business experienced a major competitive shock as a leading national brand decided to enter the market and compete with Caly's for dominance of the category. The new competitor, a well-known brand with a national footprint, is a formidable competitor. Famous for its "vast mix of flavours", the company has a formula based on counter-serve ice cream with a mix of dine-in and take-out business. When entering a new market, the new competitor maintained consistency with national pricing standards and was moderately price competitive against Caly's given its significant national purchasing power and ability to leverage a national supply network.

Carl and Ally were still perfecting their model at the time but were ready for the threat. By visiting many of their competitor's stores around the country as part of their study tour process, Carl and Ally were able to develop an understanding of what their competitor's market entry strategy would look like, how the restaurant fit-out would look, and what flavours would be on offer. As such, they were able to build a very clear picture of how their competition would behave in the local market. Additionally, since Carl and Ally were aware of the incipient competition more than a year in advance, they were able to prepare accordingly. Overall, this intelligence gave Caly's a distinctive advantage, in part because their competition underestimated Caly's as a "local" business. Carl and Ally were able to keep their loyal customers engaged by focusing on the customer experience, staying true to the core value proposition, and out-innovating the competition by offering a unique combination of flavours across the yogurt, ice cream, and gelato product platforms and with targeted promotions to keep their customers engaged. Meanwhile, while the competitor struggled to crack the student market, they were able to create a small niche focused on out-of-town travellers who wanted ice cream from a familiar brand, primarily available in supermarkets.

For the next two years, the two competitors fought bitterly for share in the market and, after a long struggle, Caly's finally prevailed. In the end, the competitive offering was not sufficiently differentiated to give customers a compelling reason to switch from Caly's and they exited the market. Caly's emerged as a stronger competitor, hardened to the competition and with a much better understanding of their customers and how their value proposition could be tuned to meet changing demands of their customers. This same dynamic repeated itself two years later with the entry of another national chain into the market and Caly's, now with a playbook for how to defeat franchise competition, was again successful, this time emerging as the dominant player in the market with close to 80% market share.

Having achieved their lofty vision and become an iconic and market-leading local business, Carl and Ally turned their attention to improving the performance of the business to enhance profitability and cash flow. One of their biggest initiatives was to acquire the property and buildings of all 11 of their shops to reduce the risk posed by loss of commercial leases and to "pay themselves" rent. This also helped them to build equity to construct their flagship shop, a modern, two-story, 5,000-square-foot building purpose-built to create an unparalleled customer experience. The new shop quickly became a "study hub" for students on the north side of town. At the advice of their accountant, Carl and Ally also vertically integrated upstream by building a small factory (large kitchen) to mix ingredients for their stores. Mixing their own ingredients helped improve profitability by bringing more margin in-house and giving Caly's the ability to create more flavour combinations. These decisions helped enhance the overall profitability of the business and provided financial security to ensure the long-term longevity of the business.

> When life looks like easy street there is danger at your door.
> – *Jerry Garcia and Robert Hunter, 1970*

When Caly's was first founded, the Internet was in its nascent stages. In the early years, Caly's offered fast and free Wi-Fi to their customers, and this proved very popular and helped establish the business as a destination for students. However, as Internet access became more ubiquitous, this became less of a differentiator. At the same time, the "experience offering" became more and more common with other restaurants; coffee houses like Starbucks in particular offered a similar proposition to Caly's and thus a substitute for students looking for somewhere new to study. Over time, students began to spend less time working together in physical spaces and more time online. These trends put pressure on Caly's top-line performance with a slow erosion of "same-store" sales over the most recent five years. To counter these trends, Carl and Ally redoubled their efforts on flavour innovation and store environment, refreshing their restaurant fit-out on a three-year cycle for all locations. This aggressive management helped to stabilise the decline, but the long-term trend worried Carl and Ally.

Another trend that Carl and Ally picked up from their frequent study tours was the introduction of self-serve yogurt to the market. The ability of consumers to mix and match flavours and toppings was becoming more popular with young people. This was particularly exciting as an opportunity to create more engagement with customers in their restaurants. Carl and Ally began to retrofit some of their restaurants with fun self-serve stations to give customers more ownership over the process and to allow for an "infinite" number of options for their customers. While this proved very popular with customers, it had little impact on top-line performance and was expensive to install and maintain alongside the counter service.

In 2016, the first FROYO, a self-serve frozen yogurt business, entered the market, down the street from Caly's original restaurant. FROYO, almost a pop-up style outlet, offered five banks of two flavours each (more than 3 million possible flavour combinations) of yogurt alongside a range of about 20 toppings. Seating for six customers on small tables was offered and the outlet had one staff member to maintain the machines and to process transactions and a total roster of three people across three shifts per restaurant. The decor in the outlet was very spartan with white subway tiled walls, bright lighting, and a stainless-steel countertop. Customers would queue into the store, fill a cup or a cone with yogurt, add their toppings, and pay by the ounce/gram at the counter based on a standard price per ounce/gram. Customers would typically purchase the yogurt for consumption outside the store there being limited seating. Overall, the typical FROYO outlet would be less than 150 square feet.

Carl and Ally, having experienced the entry of national competitors just a few years before, did not initially see FROYO as a threat. After all, Caly's was in the process of refitting its restaurants with self-serve stations and their initial market feedback was very positive. Also, the "pure" self-serve value proposition was very different from the Caly's proposition. The "in and out" convenience proposition offered by FROYO surely would not undermine the "safe place to study and eat ice cream" proposition of Caly's. In the first six months of 2016, FROYO opened five locations, often filling in alleyways between buildings or popping up in underutilised retail space.

The response

As FROYO started gaining momentum, Carl and Ally redoubled their efforts to refit their restaurants to accommodate self-serve stations alongside their traditional format in store. This process however was too slow to meet the threat and originally planned for only three restaurants per year as part of their asset refresh policy. Setting a goal to refit all of their restaurants within 18 months, Ally and Carl were confident that they could meet the threat head on. At the end of the first six months of FROYO entering the market, Caly's market share had slipped by about 10% with many Caly's customers trying the FROYO concept and liking the convenience of the format. Carl and Ally were confident, however, that their loyal customers would return once the novelty of FROYO wore off.

After the first six months, FROYO began opening up an outlet at a rate of about one per month. By the end of 2016, FROYO had ten outlets around town, many within a few metres of Caly's. Over this period, Caly's saw their market share slip an additional 10% with many locations losing money for the first time in their history. Carl and Ally finally acknowledged the threat and began an aggressive campaign to reduce costs whilst stepping up the introduction of self-serve stations and offering new flavours to entice customers to remain engaged. By the end of 2016 Caly's was in trouble, with all but one location losing money and the rate of FROYO expansion continuing to expand at one outlet per month. Carl and Ally had no choice at this point but to drastically reduce staff costs and to close the worst-performing restaurants. Product development and refit expenditure was suspended in an effort to maintain cash flow to service the debt on the property. These decisions, while necessary, undermined their value proposition. Customers began to see a drop in quality of service, further exacerbating the decline as many customers stopped coming altogether. Unfortunately, Carl and Ally were not able to sell or lease any of the property fast enough to make a difference, the typical lead time to find a tenant being six months to a year.

At 60% (and declining) market share with their existing cost structure, Caly's was no longer viable. By the end of the second calendar quarter of 2017, the business ran out of cash and had to close.

Hindsight is 2020

Over 20 years, Caly's evolved from a start-up to a market leader. The business became an iconic brand in its market and, over a very short 18 months, went from market leader to closure. How could this happen? What lessons can we draw from Caly's?

This case illustrates the typical pattern of disruption that we see across all sectors of the economy. The speed at which the decline and death of an icon can occur is not unique to Caly's. Caly's became the incumbent as both the established market leader but more importantly in mindset. The following text is an evaluation of how the incumbent mindset doomed Caly's to failure even as the insurgent, FROYO, was ascendant.

Fatal mistakes

The general awareness of Carl and Ally of their customers, competitors, and market conditions was superior to most businesses (large and small) we observe in the marketplace. Unlike many incumbents, the level of hubris and arrogance about their success was low (though not totally absent). In many ways, the rapid decline of Caly's can be described as a series of cascading failures that accumulated over time with one fatal mistake. The fatal mistake made by Carl and Ally was the failure to understand the fundamental difference between the Caly's business model and that of FROYO. As the incumbents, Carl and Ally were heavily invested in the perpetuation and defence of their existing model. When the national competition came into the market years before, Caly's was able to successfully defend their position in the market through differentiation, product innovation, and maintaining close relationships with their customers. However, while the product offering and experience were different, the business models of the national competitors were, for the most part, the same. Table 2 shows a summary comparison of Caly's vs. FROYO business models.

Having recognised the self-serve trend, Carl and Ally's response was "we can do self-serve too". The introduction of the self-serve model into their existing restaurants, while logical, shows that Carl and Ally assumed that self-serve was a customer trend alone, i.e., by offering self-serve, Caly's would satisfy this unmet customer need and maintain their position. Introduction of the self-serve format in the existing stores added additional cost and overhead

Table 2 Comparison of Caly's and FROYO Business Models

Element/assumption	Caly's	FROYO
Value proposition	"Safe place to eat and study"	"Convenient frozen yogurt"
Customer interaction	"We serve you – we are in control"	"Self-serve – customer is in control"
Store footprint	2,000–5,000 square feet	150–250 square feet
Roster	25+ people per store over three shifts	Three to four people per store over three shifts
Product	>50 flavours (yogurt/ice cream/gelato)	Ten flavours in any combination
Cost structure	High	Low
Price (x = unit price)	1.0x	.95x
Stand up time	6–12 months	1 month
Revenue/store	~$1 million	~$200K

onto an already high-cost structure. FROYO understood that Caly's cost structure was fundamentally different from theirs and exploited this weakness to their advantage by opening up new locations faster than Caly's could respond. Carl and Ally fatally assumed that their customers would not value the convenience proposition even though the pricing was roughly similar. It is important to understand that the long-term consumer trend noted above, i.e., students spending more time interacting in digital environments, also played a key role. Students were conditioned to enjoy ice cream and yogurt while studying but were increasingly willing to do this at home while interacting online with their peers. This trend, combined with self-serve, opened up the opportunity for FROYO. Had Caly's responded to the FROYO business model and not just the consumer trend, they may have had a better chance of survival. However, as the incumbent, it is unlikely that Carl and Ally would have been willing to self-cannibalise their core business. This is a frequent failing of the incumbent as we will see later in the book.

Cascading failures

As mentioned above, most incumbent organisations do their planning in one direction only, up. Caly's was no exception to this. As the business grew, Carl and Ally first prioritised store growth, then revenue, market share, and finally profit growth. Ally and Carl did not understand the "marginal economics" of their business. As growth in market share became harder and harder to achieve (after all, the marginal effort to move from 80% to 81% share would have been very high), the business *had to* refocus its efforts on internal performance (e.g., profitability) or the pursuit of adjacencies (this was not something that Carl and Ally wished to pursue). Unfortunately, very rational decisions to improve profitability, especially the acquisition of the property and, to a lesser extent, the vertical integration into ingredients mixing, reduced the business' flexibility. Carl and Ally were unaware that the business was not viable at 60% market share given their cost structure, the point at which the business collapsed. The rapid loss of share and the inability to exit underperforming restaurants (fixed cost) fast enough delivered the *coup de grace*. Modelling of a rapid share loss as part of the planning process would have given Carl and Ally more insight regarding the fragility of the business and allowed them to make decisions accordingly to make their core business model more resilient. An example of this might include a better balance of leased vs. owned premises.

Carl and Ally's inability to understand how these factors, when combined, would impact their business was only part of the story. The *incumbent mindset* played an equally important role. As market leader, Caly's inevitably overvalued its role in the market, the durability and resilience of its value proposition, and the loyalty of its customers. Carl and Ally succeeded in defending Caly's from two of the most successful national franchises in the country. It is hard to imagine not having a sense of invincibility as a result. Caly's looked very much like the Roman infantry. As the context changed, they failed to see how their model lacked sufficient robustness to adapt to the new context (in this case the introduction of FROYO to the market). Further, Carl and Ally assumed that they had time to adjust once the threat was clear. Doubling down on the existing model (cost reduction and product development enhancements) was rational but made the problem worse.

From FROYO's perspective, Caly's is a dream competitor. FROYO would have known almost exactly how Caly's would respond. The rapid rate at which they opened new locations was a deliberate attempt to force Caly's into a specific course of action. Once FROYO observed that Caly's response to self-serve was to offer this in their existing restaurants, the rest was history. The ability of FROYO to undermine Carl and Ally's key assumptions about the market was their main source of competitive advantage. FROYO would have known that not all of Caly's customers would respond to the

FROYO proposition. They only needed 20% to win. FROYO's agility and cost structure were distinct advantages. One of the key lessons from FROYO is how easily they were able to manipulate Caly's into a fatal course of action.

As a pilot, I observe that demise of Caly's resembles "controlled flight into terrain (CFIT)". Some 25% (IATA, 2018) of fatal aircraft accidents over the last 50 years can be attributed to pilot error whereby the pilot, not believing the information presented by their instruments, will ignore instrument data in favour of their instinct, assumptions, and judgement. Presented with data that does not fit their frame of reference, the pilot will literally crash the plane into a mountain, the ground, or the sea realising only in the final seconds before their fatal mistake. The incumbent is especially vulnerable to CFIT in business. Over time, incumbent businesses become less and less able to adjust to changing conditions and too often do not recognise the change until it is too late. The assumption of relative stability and overconfidence in the robustness of the business model to change are very similar to how a pilot in clear air feels moments before a disaster.

What could Carl and Ally have done differently?

As they say, hindsight is 20/20. The following are a few things that Carl and Ally might have considered as options to rescue Caly's:

(1) **Challenge assumptions** – As Caly's developed and matured as a business and withstood numerous external challenges, the assumptions that underpinned the core business became more and more absolute. These assumptions, namely that the Caly's customer would indefinitely continue to respond to their value proposition and that the conditions surrounding the business were largely stable, were never systematically challenged. These assumptions were taken as a given. Very few businesses are even aware of the assumptions upon which their business model is built much less able to fundamentally challenge these. Once the model is built and enjoys success, these "founding assumptions" tend to disappear into the background, leaving behind a business model that *must* be perpetuated. Of course, as long as the conditions surrounding the business are stable and unchanging, no problem. For established incumbent businesses, particularly big businesses, this is very difficult for a variety of reasons as we shall see later. Small businesses are no exception. Caly's founders were

still in the business and should have been aware of these assumptions and able to objectively challenge these. Confirmation bias tends to play a key role in the decision-making process of leaders. Data tends to be filtered in such a way that supports the beliefs (assumptions) of the decision makers. Only in hindsight do these become obvious. Could Carl and Ally not have identified factors that, when combined, would ultimately undermine their business model and position in the market? Maybe. The reality of running a business, in practice, leaves very little time available to pose theoretical questions about the business' key assumptions. Even when these are challenged, leaders will find a way to rationalise the *truth* of the existing assumptions. After all, the world's entire financial system came to a halt in 2008 because almost no one was willing or able to challenge the core assumption that "housing prices *always* go up". Every business rests on a small set of fundamental assumptions. All assumptions have a shelf life. Insurgents are especially adept at undermining the assumptions held by incumbents with exquisite timing.

(2) **Build a flexible architecture** – Caly's could have built more resilience into their existing business model by designing the business in such a way that it could pivot quickly if conditions change. Instead, they prioritised returns over flexibility via vertical integration and acquisition of real estate. Whatever the change, the business was not flexible enough to redeploy its resources quickly. Instead, the initial response was to "double down" on the existing formula. In some ways, Caly's was a victim of its own success. A business with 80% market share must inevitably be challenged. An operating model that allowed for a rapid retreat when conditions got tough would have been prudent. The flexibility/profit equation is one of those basic bits of analysis that never gets done. It is useful to know what the cost of a marginal unit of flexibility is in your business. It is also a useful exercise to model or game "what-if" scenarios to understand how the business would perform if severely challenged by an insurgent. Since most businesses, as I mentioned, plan only in the "up" direction, this kind of analysis seldom gets any meaningful attention.

(3) **Don't be afraid to self-cannibalise** – Had Carl and Ally understood that the FROYO model posed a fundamental challenge to the Caly's model, Carl and Ally might have introduced a model similar to the FROYO model in the market to pre-empt the FROYO market entry. Setting aside the mistake of offering self-serve yogurt inside the existing cost structure, this decision would have required self-cannibalisation of the Caly's

model and, almost certainly, would have undermined the core business. A combination of belief in the robustness of the core business model and the lack of enthusiasm to effectively damage the existing business tends to get in the way of these decisions. In the case of Caly's, this would have required significant changes to the core business (an orderly retreat) to make this successful. In practice, very few organisations are willing to self-cannibalise. Insurgents have no problem taking your market share.

(4) **Challenge your business model** – In our experience, nothing is stickier than an existing business model. Once it takes root, it is very difficult to change. The Caly's business model was ripe for disruption. Even as FROYO attacked Caly's position in the market, the response was constrained by the existing model. Reduction of cost on one hand and acceleration of product development on the other only made the problem worse. We will explore this dynamic more in the next chapter.

As with most cases of disruption, Caly's demise was avoidable and inevitable at the same time. So long as one assumes that the market conditions remain stable and the existing business is robust to future change (both conditions are necessary), disruption is inevitable. Sometimes these changes happen very slowly (changing customer behaviour) then very quickly (changing customer behaviour PLUS a new alternative in the market) owing to the compounding of key trends.

Caly's was the incumbent, weighed down by immutable assumptions and inflexibility by design. FROYO, the insurgent, unencumbered by these constraints, was able to break the "impregnable" position that Caly's created in the market in less than two years.

References

Garcia, J & Hunter, R, 1970, *Uncle John's Band, Grateful Dead*. Warner Brothers, Lyrics copyrighted by Ice Nine Publishing.

IATA, 2018, *Controlled Flight into Terrain Accident Analysis Report 2008–2017 Data*, https://www.iata.org/whatwedo/safety/Documents/cfit-report.pdf.

Merriam Webster Dictionary, 2019, viewed 13 October, 2019, https://merriam-webster.com/dictionary/insurgence.

4 | Graduation day

The birth, growth, maturity, and death of a successful business follow a relatively predictable pattern. In the early stages of development, businesses seek to find a market opportunity they can exploit and match this opportunity with a suitable business model that can be scaled to meet increasing demand. This growth pattern is typically known as the "S-Curve" based on the sigmoid function (Rogers, 1962) (see Exhibit 4). Typically, any new business selects a business model that is common to the industry and focuses on meaningful differentiation at the interface between the firm and the customer, typically through product and brand differentiation. This differentiation/value proposition (e.g., price, product, experience, etc.) defines what is unique and special about a company in the eyes of the customer. As a company develops, the value proposition evolves as the market responds favourably and rewards the firm with growth. Nothing new here.

As the firm grows, inevitable trade-offs have to be made to scale the business successfully. In order to manage the growth of a firm, an increasing degree of organisational hierarchy, division of labour, and functional specialisation is required. As firms grow ever bigger, managing complexity becomes an ever-expanding part of the management challenge. To combat complexity, the business is organised around capabilities, products (or services), markets, and customers. To maximise efficiency, processes and tasks are standardised and resources are deployed such that there is a strong balance between market opportunity and efficiency. At the core of this structure is a series of one or more business models underpinned by a set of key assumptions as we have seen earlier in the Caly's case. As long as there is available growth (a suitable market for a firm's products and services) and stability (a market context well suited to the business model), a business can scale and grow.

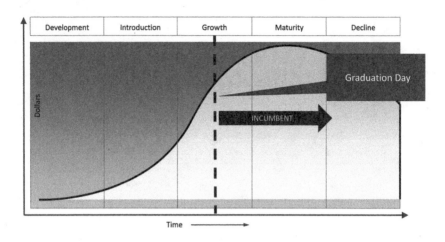

Exhibit 4 Graduation day.

Unfortunately, as the business becomes more complex and functional, the flexibility and agility of the business usually suffers as a result. Further, by design, the functionalisation of the business enshrines the business model to such an extent that it often becomes difficult, if not impossible, to change. Likewise, the assumptions underpinning that model are often forgotten or de-emphasised over time. Adding to this, the metrics, incentives, and mindset of the organisation are directed towards the efficient operation of the existing model, making leaders (including the board) and managers reluctant to challenge any core assumptions lest they undermine their own position in the firm. Inevitably, this dynamic typically leads to more and more of an internal focus and less and less focus on external market trends and customers. Again, as long as the business enjoys growth prospects and a stable context, OK. If your competitors all have the same business model, are playing by the same rules and assumptions, again, OK.

The above text describes the steady and somewhat inevitable process by which a firm becomes an incumbent. We describe this transition, the point of no return to incumbency, as the "graduation day". Following graduation to incumbency, a firm becomes progressively more vulnerable to insurgents and disruption, especially when the market context changes. In the early stages of development, a firm is relatively unburdened by organisational complexity and functional overheads. The early-stage firm has more latitude and degrees of freedom to deploy resources (albeit less resources – there is no free lunch), adjust assumptions, and make meaningful changes to their business models. Insurgents prey on the inflexibility and internal focus of incumbents. In times of stability, incumbents can erect significant barriers that can prevent insurgents from getting a beachhead. As things change however (technology, new entrants, regulation, consumer behaviour, etc.), the incumbent model becomes less defensible over time.

Typical characteristics of incumbents

The *Cambridge Dictionary* (2019) defines an incumbent as "a person or business that holds a particular position in a company, market, industry, etc. at the present time". For our purposes, an incumbent is "established" in its position and typically enjoys a strong position relative to peers in its industry. This implies some degree of market leadership, longevity, and historical durability. However, as business cycles of change continue to shorten, longevity and durability become more subjective.

Own goals

The most important characteristic of an incumbent, from our experience, is its inward-looking orientation. Incumbents tend to focus on "own goals" and optimise their own internal functional efficiency above all other things (i.e., how to do what we *already* do better, faster, and cheaper). For listed firms, the relentless pressure on short-term quarterly results and the management incentives underpinning these expectations typically reinforce this inward focus. As the incumbent grows and its position in the market becomes more mature, it becomes harder to achieve significant marginal improvement in revenue growth and market share using the same formula. Over time, the focus on profitability increases and with it the internal focus. The annual planning process reinforces this internal focus by being budget-driven rather than market-driven. In many (most?) large organisations, the budgets are set more as a function of expectations and not necessarily defined by market opportunity. As budget expectations almost always go up, leadership is forced to play it safe and focus on incremental opportunities rather than breakthrough opportunities. Thus, new opportunities are almost always judged in terms of returns relative to the existing business (i.e., ROI of new opportunities must exceed the marginal return of a unit of investment in the existing business). This approach inevitably starves new opportunities of resources in favour of the existing portfolio. Without stating the obvious, firms that are internally focused tend to be less in tune with market trends, evolving customer needs, and competition (particularly competition outside the historical field of view).

General Electric (GE), one of the world's most iconic companies of the 20th century, provides a good example of these dynamics. GE, a portfolio company holding assets (companies) from many diverse industry segments, was co-founded by Thomas Edison in the late 1800s and was an original member of the Dow Jones Industrial Average (DJIA), an elite club of high-performance industrial companies, until it was removed from the DJIA in June of 2018 (Bloomberg, 2019b). Throughout the entire 20th century, the business was recognised as one of the world's best-run companies and attracted some of the best leadership talent available. The business peaked at the turn of the 21st century with a market capitalisation of almost $600 billion, placing it amongst the world's most valuable companies at that time. Famously led by leadership guru Jack Welch, CEO of GE from 1981 to 2000, the modern GE business was built primarily through acquisition and disposal of leading businesses in sectors where GE could add value to new businesses through its ability to blueprint management discipline, harvest synergies, find cost savings, and efficiently allocate capital to generate growth using its AAA credit rating and its own bank, GE Capital, to finance growth, a key advantage. The business model was based on these advantages and was dependent on GE Capital to exquisitely time the purchase and disposal of assets and thus "paper over" the performance volatility of its industrial portfolio. This model worked for decades and delivered solid earnings growth and outstanding dividend performance. Some have even suggested that GE was a hedge fund in disguise (Arnold, 2012). Underpinning the model was a frank, almost brutal, performance culture that encouraged leaders to ruthlessly cull the bottom performers each year, retaining only the top 90% of performers.

Following the departure of Jack Welch, the business began a long and slow decline accelerated in stages by significant externalities, most notably the global financial crisis (GFC) of 2008. The GFC nearly brought GE to its knees and exposed a critical flaw in the GE business model, namely the overdependence of the business on GE Capital to generate earnings and fund investor dividends. In 2007, on the eve of the crisis, the capital division represented 55% of the company's profit (Colvin, 2018). Since the GFC, the gradual unwinding of GE Capital to reduce risk and the increase in leverage required to drive more acquisitions (many of these poorly timed or poorly executed and thus underperformers) to drive growth and maintain the GE dividend (a deeply embedded assumption) have created a sort of death spiral for GE that is difficult to break, potentially without breaking up the company itself.

Jack Welch's successor, Jeff Immelt, maintained this model well past its expiration date. As conditions changed, notably the end of the long bull market that was almost omnipresent during the Welch years, the overdependence on GE Capital as an earnings engine placing unseen risk on the company in the lead up to the GFC, the lack of availability (or acumen to procure) of the right acquisitions, and the underperformance of its industrial portfolio have placed GE in a difficult position, overleveraged and underperforming as a whole. As a result of the failure of GE to adapt to these changes, the business lost its position on the DJIA and its market capitalisation is now below $80 billion (Bloomberg, 2019a). Much of the blame can be placed on the company's culture to deliver the dividend at all costs, even if significant borrowings and/or financial engineering are required to make it happen, and its failure to challenge the historically successful model and its underlying assumptions. This trend continued through the short tenure of John Flannery until the accession of Larry Culp, current CEO, who finally cut the dividend at the start of his tenure breaking with long-standing GE tradition. The business is now undergoing an unwinding – slowly breaking up the conglomerate to emerge as a more focused and industrial-based business, back to its seemingly pre-1980 roots.

Bend don't break

Once a firm "graduates" to incumbent status, the default position in the market becomes defensive. To illustrate, in almost every sport, the leading team prioritises aggressive offence early in the game but in the final moments makes the shift to a defensive posture to hold onto their lead until the clock runs out. I believe that I have lost more hair from watching the Michigan Wolverines snatch defeat from the jaws of victory playing it safe in the fourth quarter with their legendary "bend don't break" defence than almost anything else. Incumbents, particularly market-leading incumbents, are no exception. Playing defence means, above all else, protecting what you already have. This includes, as mentioned above, the unwritten law of the incumbent "thou shalt not self-cannibalise". Unfortunately, the defensive playbook for an incumbent playing one game does not typically work against an insurgent playing another game altogether.

Apple, Inc., typifies this approach in its current form. A company previously known for its bold vision, groundbreaking new products, and "wow" factor has fallen into a pattern of harvesting the goodwill of its loyal customers, providing the minimum amount of new features and functionality to keep existing customers (barely) engaged, and relying on the exit barriers of its existing platform to prevent its customers from switching. This approach appears to have significantly diminished their ability to innovate as a company. As I write this, for example, I am using a 2013 Mac Book Pro which I have not upgraded due to the poor (and expensive) options available from Apple, the need to buy expensive peripherals, and the high cost of switching to another platform (mainly due to the thousands of photos I have in iCloud).

Keeping busy

As long as opportunities exist, incumbents are typically very good at extrapolating existing capabilities to drive growth. For example, McDonald's discovered and perfected its business model from 1955 to 1961 based on relatively cheap but tasty burgers served over the counter at high volumes. From 1961, the business was able to scale this model more or less exponentially over the next three decades reaching approximately 1,000 outlets by 1970, 10,000 outlets by the end of the 1980s, and more than 30,000 outlets by the early 2000s (Reference for Business, 2019). The scalability of the model is legendary. The basic recipe of the business didn't change for more than 40 years (forgive the pun). As a business grows and then graduates to incumbent status, these capabilities translate into strong functional silos (e.g., marketing, franchising, operations, etc.) each programmed to contribute to their part of the model efficiently, eventually becoming powerful voices inside the business, each competing for resources. As these silos mature, they too graduate to a sort of self-perpetuation status, protecting their turf and keeping busy doing what they do.

A recent example of this is the introduction of Coke Life by the Coca-Cola company. Coca-Cola, an incumbent purveyor of beverages and associated products, anchored by a 100+ year-old product, Coca-Cola, developed Coke Life in 2013 in Argentina ostensibly to offer its consumers a lower-calorie alternative to Coca-Cola with 35% fewer calories (kilojoules) and a mix of cane sugar and Stevia, a new sweetener. Given a 12-year decline in the soft drink category from 2004 to 2016 (Kell, 2017) in the Unites States, the pressure for the Coca-Cola marketing machine to introduce new products to restore growth would have been enormous. Yet the incumbent marketing organisation is designed do one thing well and that one thing over and over. One can imagine the excitement at Coca-Cola when the marketing team "discovered" that there was a previously untapped consumer segment lurking between Diet Coke and Coke Zero (no calories) on one end of the spectrum and traditional Coca-Cola on the other end (full strength). By putting a green label on the bottle or can (conveying an "on-trend" healthy and environmental image) as well as replacing "bad" high-fructose corn syrup with "good" cane sugar, the product was sure to be a hit. Alas, the product has been called the "spork" of new product introductions (a spork is part fork and part spoon) and was not a success (Murphy, 2015) never finding a market. The marketing team at Coca-Cola failed to understand that the market was evolving to functional drinks (i.e., drinks with a purpose) and away from broad "feel-good" propositions. A marketing team inside an established incumbent does what it does best, more of the same.

The Tower of Babel

The assumption of ongoing stability, lasting dominance, and an unshakeable business model is a powerful force at an incumbent firm. The temptation to exert control across the value chain and capture the associated margins and value that comes with vertical integration, done well, is highly tempting. Even the relatively low degree of vertical integration at Caly's was a good decision, until it wasn't. To be fair, not all incumbents are vertically integrated and vertical integration is a valid option for businesses under the right circumstances, even for insurgents (more on this later). However, vertical integration (the gathering of upstream or downstream stages of production into a firm) creates an additional degree of inflexibility and a further "hardening" of a firm's business model. While conditions remain constant, vertical integration can generate a tremendous amount of value. When the market context changes however, vertical integration becomes notoriously difficult to unravel.

Kodak, one of the leading industrial companies of the 20th century, was a market leader in the sale and processing of film and cameras to the consumer market (among many other things related to "coating chemistry"). Manufacturing of film and paper at scale is a highly capital-intensive business model and requires enormous economies of scale to be cost-efficient. Over decades, Kodak vertically integrated across almost the whole value chain from control of silver (raw material) and other basic chemical production (upstream) to retail, (downstream) from start to finish. This vertical integration strategy fit well with the industry dynamics of film production and was a wise choice for Kodak during most of its 100-year history, again, until it wasn't. In the mid-1970s Kodak sold an estimated 90% of all photographic film in the United States, a virtual monopoly (David Usborne, 2012), and, with the assumption that this market dominance would continue, these decisions made sense. As silver halide film technology gave way to digital imaging technology and film sales began to decline, the high degree of vertical integration made Kodak incredibly inflexible and it took decades to dismantle the company as film sales declined. Whilst the replacement of film by digital imaging was relatively slow by today's standards of disruption (the digital camera was invented by a Kodak employee (Aldred, 2016) in 1975 and it took almost 30 years for the market to displace film at scale), the degree of vertical integration at Kodak was undoubtedly a major handbrake on the transformation process at Kodak. On one hand, Kodak may not have been able to defend its incumbent market leadership without being vertically integrated, on the other the incumbent disadvantages of the resulting inflexibility associated with vertical integration created inflexibility as conditions changed.

Show me the money

One of the most powerful forces in any organisation is the incentive structure of the senior management. For incumbents, this is all about achievement of short- and long-term incentives (bonuses). For insurgents, survival is often sufficient as a reward in the short term with some real, but uncertain prospect of a significant pay-off in the future. Executives within incumbent organisations will tend to make decisions that will optimise their own short-term returns in in line with the firm's short-term objectives. This dynamic, in combination with the above factors, enshrines a high degree of caution in the incumbent firm. After all, why take the risk on a speculative innovation opportunity (e.g., digital imaging and the digital camera) that is uncertain to pay out when incremental options abound that are low-risk and provide relatively certain short-term rewards? In our experience working with many large incumbents, we often find that incentives are out of step with company strategy, often by several years, i.e., the incentives in place today are driving behaviour that represents the past far more than the future. As incumbents come under pressure from insurgents, this becomes a critical issue. Even when the response is clear, the ability of the incumbent to change focus and reorient critical behaviours is very difficult on this dimension. For incumbents that have enjoyed a significant longevity of position, some managers and leaders will have been programmed to a specific set of behaviours for decades (i.e., sell more film, digital be damned) that run counter to the firm's long-term interests.

Too big to change

In some cases, the sheer size of the incumbent firm creates a major challenge. In the case of Apple, as mentioned above, one of its major problems looking ahead is its ability to find opportunities that can move the dial at scale. At the time of writing, Apple, Inc., turns over more than $250 billion (Statista, 2019). Apple routinely divests product lines in the $billions, presumably because of a high degree of discipline required to focus on high-value product lines (smartphones in particular). Finding a new product line that will deliver greater than $5 billion (i.e., a material impact) of revenue is very difficult to achieve without a major shift in a firm's business model. It is however possible. For example, Amazon was successful in building Amazon Web Services (AWS) into a >$25 billion business on top of its retail business. Apple has not been able to find incremental growth at that scale, though it's services business (apps, music, Apple Care, etc.) has become the key engine of growth as consumer electronic products mature, but these are already a key part of the existing business model. The majority of these revenues (>$11 billion per quarter) are generated from Apple's platform businesses. Where will Apple find enough revenue to make a difference? Rumours abound about television (late to the party with Apple TV+?), health, education, transportation, etc. As the core business peaks, Apple's biggest challenge as an incumbent will be to replace these revenues on a scale that makes a material difference without eroding the brand. In the case of Kodak, this proved impossible. The film business was just too big and too profitable, until it wasn't. Kodak was unable to find a material replacement for the core film business as the transition to digital washed over them. In spite of having an almost legendary innovation engine (albeit slow and unfocused), Kodak could not find ways to innovate their business model into new (digital) domains. Will Apple make the same mistake?

Thou shalt not self-cannibalise

As new and disruptive opportunities emerge for incumbents, a dilemma arises. Should the firm work against itself and embrace new opportunities at the expense of the core business? The answer is often "no". The default position of the incumbent is to maintain and extend, not replace. The pressure on executives to keep the existing business at peak performance (i.e., driving up revenues and margins) is enormous. This creates a relatively conservative risk profile. The instinct to avoid self-cannibalisation is multifaceted. Setting aside the pressure to perform, timing plays an important role. Unfortunately, the ramp up of new sources of revenue and profit rarely matches the profile of current profit engines in scale or in quality. As such, managers face a high degree of uncertainty regarding how aggressively to challenge their own products in the market. Being too aggressive tends to water down performance in the short term and not aggressive enough will impact the firm's ability to compete in the future. Walking this razor's edge is difficult enough in stable contexts but much more difficult to read when a fundamental shift is underway. Organisational structure and the internal power structure can play a role as well. Product or division managers with key legacy products are incentivised and "tribally programmed" to protect their turf and compete for resources. As products and existing business models begin to mature, these leaders inevitably put forward aggressive business cases to "restore growth" even as customers have moved on. These cases tend to get more attention than the nascent growth opportunity business cases and therefore more resources, often because of the power controlled by leaders of legacy lines of business. Finally, few incumbent businesses are particularly rigorous in their portfolio and lifecycle management processes. It is incredibly difficult to "stop doing" things that have momentum (e.g., kill off low-performing stock-keeping units (SKUs) or product lines as new ones come on stream for fear of losing an inch of revenue or profitability). As a result, "zombie" projects and products stay on the books far past their use-by date. All of these factors contribute to the unwritten rule "thou shalt not self-cannibalise". The net result of all of these factors is further lack of speed and flexibility. When change comes along, most firms hang on too long and often too late.

In 2017 (Yu, 2016), Apple was particularly ruthless in killing off the iPod in favour of the iPhone as smartphone ubiquity made the iPod functionality mostly redundant (for my own purposes, I wish they had kept it). I bought a bag full of iPod Nanos when that product was discontinued, mostly for running, as I find the iPhone too bulky to run with. A much-loved product was discontinued. Fast-forward to today and the fear of self-cannibalisation of the Mac range with the iPad seems to have prevented Apple from enabling certain functionality (e.g., mouse support) as a main feature in the iPad. As such, the iPad remains primarily a consumption device when it comes to text. This policy has left Apple open to insurgent competition from Microsoft (more on this later) with the Surface range. It seems, from an outside perspective, that this is strong evidence that Apple is in the process of "graduation" and has become more cautious with self-cannibalisation in recent years.

Jump the queue

Of course, some incumbents are successful in adapting to change. Why take the risk and develop new business models and disruptive products when these can be purchased, making the founders of the (formerly) insurgent firm fabulously wealthy in the bargain? Big firms gobbling up smaller more nimble firms is a tried and tested way to jump the queue and hedge bets across a number of opportunities. However, research suggests (Godfred Koi-Akrofi, July 2016) that between 50% and 80% of mergers and acquisitions (M&A) fail to achieve desired results. Given that the majority of M&A activity is initiated and consummated by incumbents, the track record of firms trying to buy into disruption is hardly impressive. Incumbents are notoriously poor at buying firms that are anything other than a carbon copy of the existing business. There are many reasons for this, but the main one is that the incumbent firm is typically solving for something different than the insurgent firm and, as a result, the cultures, incentives, risk profiles, power structures, etc., all contribute to failure as these inevitably come into conflict. It is difficult for an incumbent to buy an insurgent firm without ruining it outright, though not impossible. Purchasing an insurgent that is particularly aggressive in disrupting the existing model can have a defensive silver lining and can act as a hedge against future disruption. Taking players off the board before they reach scale can be an effective way of shoring up an incumbent firm's defences in the short term. Famously, Blockbuster turned down the acquisition of Netflix in its early stages of development for $50 million (2000), a paltry sum for Blockbuster at the time (Chong, 2015). However, one wonders if Blockbuster CEO, John Antioco, was canny in his decision knowing that Blockbuster, the then incumbent, would not have been able to successfully merge Netflix into the Blockbuster empire (more on that later).

Piggy in the middle

Given the choice of being an incumbent in a stable market or an insurgent in a turbulent market, it is easy to justify the choices that incumbents make to maintain and grow their existing position, focus internally, and continue to do more of the same. The problem is, like the proverbial frog in the beaker of slowly boiling water, the incumbent almost never recognises AND acts (the "and" is important) on the change in context until it is too late. Superior ("fortified") incumbents (Apple, Coca-Cola, etc.) are better insulated than their smaller rivals (i.e., inferior or "vulnerable" incumbents) to weather small changes in context owing to their vast resources, brand loyalty, and strong market position. Incumbent firms caught in the middle between fortified incumbents and aggressive insurgents in unstable market contexts are particularly vulnerable. Higher education is a great example. As the needs of employers change (e.g., automation, AI, etc.) colliding with changing preferences of the workforce (e.g., "gig" economy, portfolio careers, etc.) and demographic changes, there is a slow but real "crunch" in the middle-market liberal education institutions as digital alternatives emerge with new business models and fortified incumbents (e.g., Cambridge, Harvard, etc.) aggressively defend their positions. The institutions in the middle are unable to adapt and are beginning to exit the market, some of these institutions with decades (or more) of history (Horn, 2018). The lesson? Don't get caught in the middle. If you are not a fortified incumbent and protected by a singularly important brand, endowment, capability, patent, or regulatory protection, you will eventually be crushed between disruptive forces on one end of the spectrum and fortified incumbents on the other (Exhibit 5).

Insurgents are different

In contrast to the world of the incumbent as described above, the world of the insurgent is different. Insurgents cannot hope to dislodge established "fortified" incumbents by playing the same game on the same board with the same rules. Insurgents must look to find opportunity in unstable markets where incumbents are "slow, lazy, fat and happy". The good news is that both conditions for success exist in almost every industry (i.e., instability, unsatisfied customers and lazy incumbents). There is a misconception that insurgents are always start-ups. While true in some cases, this is not always true. Insurgence is a mindset more than a position on the S-curve, though the

Exhibit 5 Don't get caught in the middle.

characteristics of insurgence are more often found in early-stage businesses than later-stage businesses. One of the themes of this book is to make the case that established firms can behave like insurgents at scale. Looking at the characteristics of the incumbent as described above, one might assume that the insurgent is simply the opposite of the incumbent. For the most part, this is true.

A defining characteristic

In our experience, the principal characteristic of the insurgent is what we describe as "Customer and Market Proximity". Insurgent firms are much closer to their customers and the market context than incumbent firms (see Exhibit 6). As such, they tend to manage their businesses more from the out-side-in than the inside-out. Customer proximity refers to how close the firm is (i.e., how proximate) to understanding the needs of customers and consumers and the ability of the firm to orbit the customer (all things serve the needs of customers). Market proximity refers to how well the firm understands converging trends in the market. An insurgent firm will typically have a deep

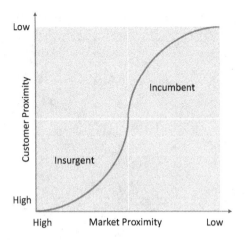

Exhibit 6 Customer and market proximity.

connection on both of these issues and importantly will be able to create business models that simultaneously exploit opportunities to serve emerging needs of customers whilst capturing opportunities presented by emergent trends. Importantly, insurgents take nothing for granted in this pursuit and are willing and able to pivot almost continuously, even to the extent of tearing up existing models and rewriting them on the fly to take advantage of emerging needs. Because insurgents are often pursuing, at least initially, opportunities that are perceived as sub-scale by incumbents, this experimentation can evolve through multiple cycles before becoming noticed by incumbents.

Playing a different game

Insurgents are programmed to avoid playing on incumbent's home turf. Successful insurgents almost always find a way to play a fundamentally different game with different rules, assumptions, and, above all, a different (even subtly so) business model. The models and assumptions governing established incumbents are surprisingly transparent and easy to identify. Once these are known, it becomes relatively easy to find and exploit the weaknesses presented by the established incumbent if one is inclined to do so.

Netflix, in its original predigital mail order configuration, was designed to exploit a critical weakness presented by the then incumbent, Blockbuster. Blockbuster, a firm based on a retail over-the-counter video rental business model, was heavily reliant on late fees as a key engine of their profitability

(Salem-Baskin, 2013) and was built on the key assumption that consumers were predominantly interested in browsing titles in-store (after all, this model successfully bridged the gap from VHS to DVD format). Netflix deliberately exploited these two fundamental parts of the Blockbuster business model by introducing a model that eliminated both late fees and the in-store browsing experience in favour of a catalogue-based subscription model whereby DVDs would be supplied to consumers via mail order on a monthly basis with no late fees (so long as the previous month's video was returned new ones could be shipped). Netflix, being customer-proximate, understood that customers *hated* late fees and that Blockbuster's model was dependent on late fees to be successful (late fees represented 16% of revenue in 2000) (Anderson and Liedtke, 2010). A critical weakness. Netflix also understood that the market was unstable and that over time, the DVD was a "transition technology" that would give way to digital streaming once the convergence of processing power, cheap memory, and superfast broadband reached the mainstream. In short, Netflix created an alternative business model that struck at the heart of the key weakness of the incumbent and, at the same time, was resilient to the future. It is well known that Blockbuster was not resilient to changes in consumer and market change (i.e., their business model was not robust to the changes in the market) and, of course, Netflix has become a market leader in video subscriptions and original content (more on this later).

Sometimes a would-be insurgent fails to unseat an incumbent by failing to apply the above principles. In 2011, Masters Home Improvement, a joint venture between Woolworths, an Australian grocery chain, and Lowes, an American hardware chain, came together to enter the Australian market and challenge the dominant incumbent, Bunnings. The core assumptions made by Masters appear to have been that the Australian market had broadly similar characteristics to the market in the United States (i.e., the popularity of "do-it-yourself"), that consumers were unsatisfied by the incumbent (Bunnings) experience, and that the market had room for another player that could occupy the market in an eventual duopoly (similar to the Home Depot and Lowe's duopoly in the United States). The core model for Masters was nearly identical to Bunnings (with the exception of a nascent online store offered by Masters) with Masters offering a big-box retail model based on "everyday low prices" in metro and suburban markets near capital cities. This model was fundamentally the same as Bunnings. Masters eventually opened more than 60 stores (Evans, 2016) but never turned a profit and the offering did not resonate with consumers.

45

Masters was a would-be insurgent that acted like an incumbent. Masters offered the same model with the same assumptions whilst entering a relatively stable market occupied by a fortified incumbent. It was a disaster. Bunnings had little trouble defending the market against Masters. Bunnings superior bargaining power with suppliers meant that Masters was unable to provide many products and brands that consumers expected to see in a hardware store and ended up with an inferior range (i.e., inferior product selection). Masters was also unable to sufficiently differentiate the customer experience (Masters was not customer-proximate) from Bunnings and customers frequently complained about the Masters in-store service experience (Chung, 2016). The critical point of failure was not one of bad execution so much as bad strategy. Masters was built on assumptions that were not consistent with the market, customer, and competitive dynamics. The business model of Masters was undifferentiated from that of Bunnings and the customer experience was also inferior to Bunnings offer. This is what often happens when the incumbent tries to become the insurgent without fully understanding the above rules of thumb, i.e., exploit unstable market conditions, undermine incumbent's key assumptions, focus on customer and market proximity, and develop an alternative business model governed by a different set of rules. In the Masters case, the market was *stable* and the incumbent was well-fortified and well-entrenched. Had Masters created some market instability or created a business model that was able to undermine a critical core assumption of Bunnings, the story may have turned out differently.

These principles appear in almost every case of disruption that we are aware of. Later on, we will expand these core principles.

References

Aldred, J, 2016, The world's first digital camera, introduced by the man who invented it, viewed 18 August 2019, https://diyphotography.net/worlds-first-digital-camera-introduced-man-invented/.

Anderson, M & Liedtke, M, 2010, Hubris – and late fees – doomed Blockbuster, http://nbcnews.com/id/39332696/ns/business-retail/t/hubris-late-fees-doomed-blockbuster.

Arnold, J, 2012, GE: a hedge fund in disguise, viewed 16 August 2019, https://seekingalpha.com/article/1087631-ge-a-hedge-fund-in-disguise.

Bloomberg, 2019a, viewed 18 August 2019, https://bloomberg.com/profile/company/GE:US.

Bloomberg, 2019b, Charting GE's historic rise and tortured downfall, viewed 16 August 2019, https://bloomberg.com/graphics/2019-general-electric-rise-and-downfall/.

Cambridge Dictionary, https://dictionary.cambridge.org/dictionary/english/incumbent.

Chong, C, 2015, Blockbuster's CEO once passed up a chance to buy Netflix for only $50 million, viewed 18 August 2019, https://businessinsider.com.au/blockbuster-ceo-passed-up-chance-to-buy-netflix-for-50-million-2015-7?r=US&IR=T.

Chung, F, 2016, 'Not as good as Bunnings', https://news.com.au/finance/business/retail/not-as-good-as-bunnings/news-story/b23138da9b6917f7af17b628d01818df.

Colvin, G, 2018, What the hell happened at GE?: few corporate meltdowns have been as swift and dramatic as General Electric's over the past 18 months – but the problems started long before that, viewed 16 August 2019, https://fortune.com/longform/ge-decline-what-the-hell-happened/.

Evans, S, 2016, What went wrong at Wollworths' Masters?, viewed 18 August 19, https://afr.com/business/what-went-wrong-at-woolworths-masters-20160118-gm7y65.

Horn, M, 2018, Will half of all colleges really close in the next decade?, viewed 18 August 2019, https://forbes.com/sites/michaelhorn/2018/12/13/will-half-of-all-colleges-really-close-in-the-next-decade/#65267ba552e5.

Kell, J, 2017, viewed 18 August 2019, https://fortune.com/2017/04/19/coca-cola-pepsi-dr-pepper-soda-water.

Koi-Acrofi, Mergers and acquisitions failure rates and perspectives on why they fail, *International Journal of Innovation and Applied Studies*, vol. 17, no. 1, pp. 150–158.

Murphy, J, 2015, Spork life: dysfunction at the heart of Coca-Cola, viewed 18 August 2019, https://news.com.au/finance/business/other-industries/spork-life-dysfunction-at-the-heart-of-cocacola/news-story/e02d21493c23b58c4ff48bb96cbb3de7>.

Reference for Business, 2019, McDonald's corporation – company profile, information, business description, history, background information on McDonald's corporation, viewed 18 August 2019, https://referenceforbusiness.com/history2/56/McDonald-s-Corporation.html.

Rogers, E, 1962, *Diffusion of Innovations*, 5th ed. Free Press, Glencoe.

Salem-Baskin, J, 2013, The internet didn't kill Blockbuster, the company did it to itself, viewed 18 August 2019, https://forbes.com/sites/jonathansalembaskin/2013/11/08/the-internet-didnt-kill-9blockbuster-the-company-did-it-to-itself/#467e48fb6488.

Statista, Technology & telecommunications/consumer electronics/Apple: revenue worldwide 2004–2018, viewed 16 August 2019, https://statista.com/statistics/265125/total-net-sales-of-apple-since-2004/.

Usborne, D, 2012, The moment it all went wrong for Kodak, viewed 18 August 2019, https://independent.co.uk/news/business/analysis-and-features/the-moment-it-all-went-wrong-for-kodak-6292212.html.

Yu, H, 2016, Apple's dwindling sales show importance of self-cannibalization, viewed 16 August 2019, https://imd.org/research-knowledge/articles/apples-dwindling-sales-show-importance-of-self-cannibalization.

The Insurgence framework – the Y-axis

In the next several chapters, we will outline a framework to illustrate how the behaviour and choices made by incumbents and insurgents differ according to their predisposition, mindset, and opportunities. This framework has been field tested and reviewed with hundreds of CEOs and functional managers from both incumbent and insurgent organisations alike. Our goal is to provide leaders with a way to think about strategy design in unstable market contexts and to help them understand how, in the case of incumbents, to combat (or initiate insurgence) insurgents and, in the case of insurgents, better understand how to deliberately undermine the position of incumbents in the markets. We do not believe that the difference between incumbents and insurgents is binary; however, as mentioned above, it is typically very difficult for incumbents to occupy a dual role once "graduation" has been achieved. We will then apply this framework to several case examples to illustrate how different organisations in incumbent and insurgent domains typically behave.

The framework itself is very simple and can be plotted on a matrix comprised of an X- and Y-axis (see Exhibit 7). The Y-axis represents, broadly, the space in the market occupied by a firm and the X-axis represents the predominant business model that the firm employs in the market. We will explore the Y-axis in this chapter and the X-axis in the following chapter. We fully recognise that a firm may have more than one business model and, as such, we choose to use this as the basic unit of analysis rather than a division or a market. The purpose of this model is to show how incumbents and insurgents behave and to provide a basic model to describe how disruption typically unfolds.

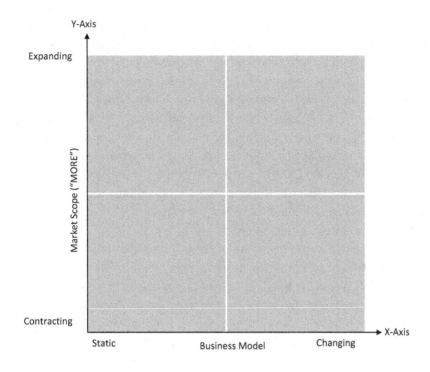

Exhibit 7 Insurgence framework.

Y-axis

The Y-axis of the framework is what we describe as the "more" axis. To explain, consider the options available to the incumbent firm in delivering growth. As mentioned above, annual planning and budgeting, particularly in large organisations, inevitably requires managers to deliver ever more growth, profit, market share, etc. Rarely, especially in times of market stability, do expectations go in the opposite direction (i.e., in my relatively long career, I have not often seen a board set the expectation for a business to achieve "less"). Once a target is established, typically in terms of revenue, profit, and sometimes market share (though often not), the challenge set before the leadership team is to determine how to achieve that target. A gap will always exist between current and expected future performance that needs to be bridged by incremental activity. As such, the planning process will usually precipitate a set of objectives and initiatives for closing this gap. Ideally, the strategy is designed to identify where the most fertile opportunities exist for a

49

firm that capitalise on the firm's strengths in the market relative to customers and competitors. As mentioned in Chapter 2, most firms skip the strategy part and focus instead on the objectives and the question: "how can we achieve the target?" Usually, the output of the planning process includes a vision statement (what do we want to be in the future as a firm), a SWOT assessment (strengths, weaknesses, opportunities, threats), and the identification of a series of objectives that communicate how the organisation will operationalise the vision. Eventually, a series of initiatives or projects will be agreed and a budget allocated to fuel the pursuit of these initiatives (i.e., "more"). This is the predominant *stable market* strategy design process for most firms, with some nuance here and there and the employment of other tools and templates to answer specific questions along the way.

It is surprising how few levers are available for leaders to pull in the pursuit of "more". From a revenue growth perspective, there are five predominant levers. Pulling any of the levers will help a firm move up the Y-axis (assuming the firm wants "more", otherwise the firm may move down the Y-axis). The following describes each lever in turn. More often than not, these levers are pulled simultaneously and not in isolation. Once this is understood, much of the mystery surrounding strategy (at least in stable markets) can be removed (Exhibit 8).

New products and services

Without stating the obvious, the introduction of new products and services represents one option for leaders to drive growth (i.e., achieve "more"). For incumbent firms, this typically means creating new variations on existing products and services and occasionally the introduction of something entirely new. In practice, the majority of new product introductions are of the former type. To give an example, the introduction of Coke Life was a new product introduction that was essentially a line extension of an existing product (Coca-Cola). This product would have had significant budget expectations in terms of contribution to revenue, profit, and market share, one can assume. The original iPhone introduced by Apple in 2007 was an example of a new product and the subsequent models from that point to today have been improvements and refinements on the original model. The same applies to services. A tax accounting firm will introduce new services to clients as the tax code changes or their client needs evolve perhaps bridging the gap

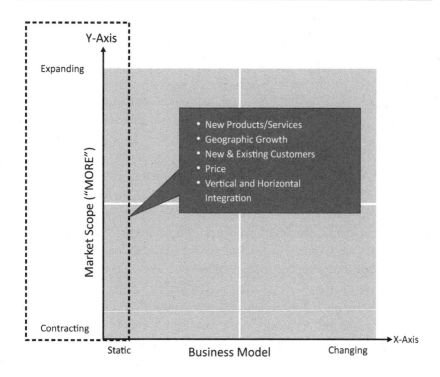

Exhibit 8 Y-axis.

between personal and business tax services for a client. In the Caly's case we studied in Chapter 3, the introduction of new flavours and categories over time (i.e., from yogurt to ice cream and then gelato) represented their product growth focus. Over time, incumbent firms build up barriers for would-be insurgents by creating brands (e.g., Apple, Coca-Cola, etc.), pouring significant resources into research and development, building up customer loyalty, etc. These barriers make it easier for incumbents to invest incrementally in existing product platforms and harder for insurgents to break in. We estimate that 80% or more of a firm's innovation resources on average are deployed to product development (innovation). In short, leaders will almost always pull the product/service lever to drive growth (moving upwards on the Y-axis). It is worth noting that to be successful in the introduction of a new product, at least two conditions are required. First, some customer or consumer sees value in the product and wishes to purchase that product. Second, that product must be sufficiently differentiated from the competition (price, value, etc.). Often products are introduced without sufficient data to support these conditions.

Geographic growth

Another key Y-axis variable is geography. A firm, having established a product that is well received in one market, will typically attempt to extrapolate that success in new markets. This makes sense and digital marketplaces make geographic growth available to small and large firms alike. Having discovered a product formula that has legs, a firm almost always seeks to identify and exploit new markets, whether adjacent geographically to where the current products are sold (note we are using products and services interchangeably here) or in far-flung markets on the other side of the world. The trick with geographic growth is to be able to find customers that are keen to buy your products and identify markets that are not too saturated with existing competition. In the Caly's case, we saw that once the market they were interested in, Ann Arbor, was saturated, they deliberately did not attempt to grow outside this boundary for fear of adding additional management complexity. McDonald's, on the other hand, having discovered a successful recipe in the early 1960s, was able to grow for decades using a largely standard product offered in ever more jurisdictions. Geographic growth is always an option for firms to drive growth. The difficult choice is where and how to capture this growth and the eventual management of the complexity associated with managing geographic growth.

New and existing customers

All firms derive their growth from customers; however, incumbent firms often retreat away from customers over time, instead prioritising growth from products. Of course, customers buy the products, but the point being made is that the opportunities to find new customers or sell more to existing customers is a key growth lever for most firms but many firms lack insight into this simple idea and do not prioritise a deep understanding of their customer's needs. Finding new customer segments for existing products and services and ways to open up existing customer relationships (i.e., get customers to buy more of your stuff) is a key Y-axis variable. For example, Lego, traditionally targeted at boys between the ages of 6 and 11, has, in recent years, been very successful in identification of, and focus on, growth in other segments including young girls, women, teachers, artists, engineers, etc. Professional services firms (e.g., accountants, lawyers, consultants) derive much of their growth from "trusted adviser" relationships seeking to be available to help clients navigate ever more challenges. As it is easier and less costly to leverage existing customer relationships than it is to develop new ones, firms become more and more focused on building and expanding existing relationships often using customer relationship management and digital marketing automation software to support their efforts.

Price

A firm can drive both revenue and profit growth from passing on price increases to customers. While this is not necessarily a sustainable growth strategy, price increases are a legitimate growth mechanism and another way to move along the Y-axis. Firms will typically increase prices annually to reflect rising input costs or in cases where demand for the firm's products is greater than supply. Price increases can also be used to send a signal to the market and influence behaviours. Incumbent firms with few of the above opportunities (product/customer/geography) will often use price as an option of last resort to drive temporary growth. Successful price increases assume that the market for a product is relatively inelastic (i.e., customers will accept the price increases without defecting to alternatives). Apple has been very successful in recent years in using aggressive price increases to drive value in an otherwise saturated market for handsets by increasing prices for new models or offering laptop products with limited (fewer than previous models) features that require the purchase of peripherals such as dongles, effectively increasing the price for consumers. This is possible because of the strong brand loyalty that customers have for Apple's products (highly inelastic) and the relatively high cost of switching, creating a barrier for customers to switch to other platforms. Some products grow, precisely because they are expensive (e.g., luxury goods like watches, yachts, performance cars). These products are known as Veblen goods (Chen, 2019) after the American economist Thorstein Veblen, who, reportedly, first noticed that some products have an upward-sloping demand curve. For most firms outside of those providing luxury goods, their products will not behave this way and will have more typical downward-sloping demand curves that trade-off price and demand (i.e., price increases will eventually have a negative demand consequence).

Vertical and horizontal integration

The final of the five levers available to firms is to grow into vertical or horizontal adjacencies. Vertical adjacencies were described in Chapter 3 when we showed that Caly's moved upstream to capture additional growth by opening up an ingredient factory. As firms grow, this becomes a more attractive option. Recently on a trip to Queenstown, New Zealand, it was observed that a popular (and delicious) hamburger joint, Fergburger, had, since the author's previous trip, opened a bakery adjacent to the original hamburger joint that both provided freshly baked goods but also baked the buns for the hamburger joint (which typically had long queues and is highly in demand in Queenstown). Manufacture of the buns represents a vertical integration, and the use of bakery capability and capacity to sell other baked goods is an example of a horizontal adjacency. Incidentally, the next shop over from the bakery contains Mrs. Ferg, which sells ice cream, another horizontal adjacency. Firms can move along the Y-axis by finding and extrapolating capabilities into vertical or horizontal spaces (the bakery goods) or they can move upstream or downstream to control production (the burger buns) or distribution (delivery). Firms both large and small employ this method for growth. Virgin Group famously pursues adjacent markets where the brand and the

Exhibit 9 Fergburger.

business system can be employed in markets that on their face are not related in any meaningful way (e.g., music and airlines). In the case of Virgin, the brand is the capability that is being extrapolated (Exhibit 9).

The above levers are well known to almost every reader and found in nearly every strategy. The insight here is that there are *only* five major levers and used in any combination represent the growth formula for the majority of firms. Standing back from every strategy I have observed directly or indirectly, it is always the same few variables. Incumbents in particular are masters of pulling these levers. Incumbents tend to focus on extrapolative growth, seeking always to squeeze existing capabilities in new ways to enhance growth through one or more of the five levers. We refer to this as "Y-axis" growth. As incumbents mature and fewer opportunities exist for Y-axis growth, and as markets become increasingly unstable, performance begins to stall, prompting firms to look inward for ways to reduce cost and complexity, thereby prioritising profits over revenue growth. All firms at one point or another travel up (and sometimes down) the Y-axis.

Reference

Chen, J, 2019, Veblen good, *Economics*, viewed 18 August 2019, https://investopedia .com/terms/v/veblen-good.asp.

The Insurgence framework – the X-axis

All firms, incumbents, and insurgents, alike, have, at their core, one or more business model(s) fuelling their efforts in the market. A firm's business model represents that firm's unique recipe to create, capture, and deliver value (Osterwalder and Pigneur, 2010). A firm may simultaneously operate many business models (consider General Electric, a multi-business company competing in diverse markets (lighting, radios, aircraft engines, etc.) each serving a different market). The recipe itself is unique to the firm, but some firms apply standardised business models representative of an industry, wherein most or all of the businesses in that industry have a more or less common business model. For our purposes, we place the business model of the firm on the X-axis of the Insurgence framework and travelling across the X-axis is representative of a material change in the recipe of a firm's business model, for example, by changing the distribution model and how the firm captures value from consumers. There has been much written about business models in recent years, so we will be brief in describing what a business model is and its typical ingredients. All business models have one thing in common, value creation, however defined. For example, a not-for-profit firm focused on caring for the ageing may have a business model that delivers value for clients in terms of health outcomes with only secondary consideration to generating funds. Equally, a for-profit, publicly traded firm may define value only in terms of shareholder value (i.e., total shareholder returns or TSR). All business models produce a value outcome depending on the purpose of the business. It should not be assumed that value is always equal to a monetary or shareholder outcome.

Overall, a business model can be viewed as the highest-level company process or framework that delivers an outcome for customers. A business model converts inputs on the supply side (e.g., raw materials, information, etc.) into outputs on the demand side that are eventually converted into value for customers (e.g., products, services, etc.). On the supply side (inside and upstream of the firm), a firm seeks to configure its resources efficiently to convert inputs to outputs and value via a network of internal and external capabilities and stakeholders (e.g., suppliers, partners, etc.). These capabilities are configured in such a way that they fuel the firm's value creation efforts. On the demand side (at the interface with the customer and outside/downstream of the firm), a firm deploys resources to get its goods and services to market in such a way that the customer can access them (e.g., distribution) and that conveys the unique properties of the goods and services themselves (i.e., the firm's value proposition). This includes the selling model, marketing, distribution channels, customer experience, etc. In addition to demand and supply side factors, the business model will include *how* the firm engages with customers to create economic (or other) value (i.e., how it spends and makes money and transacts with customers). For example, one accounting firm may prefer to charge a fixed fee for service to prepare your tax return and another may prefer to charge you by the hour. This is a simple example of how a firm translates its recipe into, in this case, economic value by altering a key element of the business model. There are numerous methods available to illustrate and document business models, the most widely used being the Business Model Canvas (Strategyzer, 2019), though we prefer more visual means of communicating the flow of value amongst stakeholders in a system. In short, a business model brings together four component parts: 1) operating model, 2) go-to-market model, 3) economic model, and 4) value proposition.

Business models can combine an almost infinite number of factors and can be incredibly simple or enormously complex. In the Caly's case, we observed two alternative business models, each ultimately delivering a similar product to a consumer. However, the means of making that happen varied significantly in terms of customer experience, delivery of product, footprint, cost structure, etc. The key insight from the case was that the introduction of an alternative business model that presented a different way of creating value for customers, on a fundamentally different cost curve, was what unravelled Caly's hold on the market. Had Caly's made a significant change to its existing business model on any of the dimensions described above, this would have been a move along the X-axis in our framework. Caly's competitor can be viewed as an X-axis competitor having outcompeted Caly's by offering a materially different business model. Insurgents are, more often than not, X-axis competitors. See Chapter 3, Table 2, for a comparison of Caly's and FROYO business models.

Once a firm discovers and "perfects" a business model, the typical goal is to perpetuate and protect that model to extract as much value from the model over time as possible. In some cases, a business model will maintain relevance over decades (or even centuries), and in others it may last only a short time. The sustainability of a given business model is generally an important consideration for the designer of that model and the subsequent management that is charged with ongoing stewardship of that model. Generally, once a business model has been created and has demonstrated some success in a given market context, that model can operate effectively indefinitely under the following conditions: 1) customers/consumers continue to value the output of the model, 2) market context is relatively stable, 3) there is no competing alternative model, and 4) there is room for growth driven by one or more Y-axis variables (e.g., price, geography, customer segment, product, adjacency). When any of these conditions change significantly, a business model becomes vulnerable.

One of the most interesting things about business models is how invisible they are to incumbent firms. Once the business model is created and perfected, it is very often forgotten or relegated to the background. In our work, we have asked executives in countless firms (public and private sector) to communicate or illustrate their business models to better understand their recipe for creating value. Most are unable to communicate their business models cogently and some look at us with blank stares as if they never paid the question a moment's notice. This applies more often to incumbents than insurgents to be sure. Why would a firm's leaders lose sight of something so important? Our theory is that the leaders of most firms inherit the business model from previous generations of leadership along with an unspoken contract to maintain and grow the existing business model (i.e., hold the X-axis constant, focus on the Y-axis) without making material changes. An incentive package to reinforce this contract (see above) is almost always in place.

From my own experience, I recall that being hired into an existing firm (i.e., a going concern) comes with an expectation of doing "more" but not tinkering with the underlying recipe (without being met with a degree of resistance and scorn). Additionally, once the business model is cast in stone it is incredibly difficult to change, so why bother? As incumbents mature and become more functionally oriented and "inside-out" in their mindset, the business model becomes almost completely opaque to functional management inside the organisation who are also incentivised to operate their own small part of the overall model. Most functional managers have little or no visibility to the whole business model and are tasked only to perform their duties inside the construct of the current model. In other words, the existing business model becomes almost immutable over time. In the meantime, the assumptions that underpin that business model recede into distant memory becoming forgotten and almost never tested unless there is a major shock or disruption threatening the firm. Afterall, almost no one confronted the assumption that housing prices would always go up in the lead up to the global financial crisis (GFC). This "underlying assumption" was left unchallenged and was a major contributor to the collapse of the global economic model in the 2008 GFC (Duca, 2010) In a nutshell, most firms will HOLD THEIR BUSINESS MODELS CONSTANT and not materially alter their models under even the direst circumstances. Incumbent firms tend to fix their position on the X-axis and tend only to focus on Y-axis variables, even (maybe especially) in times of significant changing context (Exhibit 10).

In this respect, the Caly's case is identical to the Kodak case, the Blockbuster case, and almost every disruption case we are aware of. The fatal mistake of the incumbent is to continue to tinker on the Y-axis while the insurgent attacks on the X-axis. By the time the incumbent firm realises what is happening, it's too late to change or the resistance to change is so great that the incumbent is unable to act.

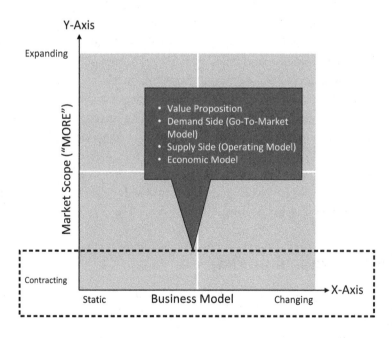

Exhibit 10 X-axis.

Returning to the Blockbuster and Netflix case, let's use this case to illustrate the point by first illustrating the business models of each firm in turn.

Blockbuster business model

Blockbuster, as briefly mentioned in Chapter 4, was a retail video rental firm. The basic premise of the model was that Blockbuster would license video titles (movies and television content) from the studios (e.g., Disney) to make their content available to consumers on a particular media (VHS, DVD, etc.) for a rental fee. Typically, the rental agreement would include a discount for multiple titles rented at the same time. Consumers would rent the videos for a fixed duration (typically 24 hours to 7 days) and, if returned late, would be charged a late fee per day (at its peak in 2000, Blockbuster generated US$800 million in late fees representing 16% of sales) (Leopold, 2013). Rentals would occur in a video store located in a convenient urban or suburban location, where customers would browse the collection of movies and, eventually, select a title. Typically, during the first contact, the customer would sign up for a Blockbuster "membership", provide essential data (driver's licence, credit card details), and pay a small membership fee. Blockbuster had a mix of company-owned and franchise outlets in the United States and internationally. At the end of the chain of activities delivered by Blockbuster, the outcome for the customer was to enjoy the video at home, perhaps also having purchased some retail items from Blockbuster along the way (popcorn, soda, candy, etc.). Blockbuster was focused on providing the latest titles for consumers with a high rate of availability. As a leading incumbent, Blockbuster was able to leverage its market power to ensure adequate supply of new titles in sufficient quantity to ensure that these titles would not "stock-out" too often (i.e., the titles would be available to consumers for hot content). At its peak, Blockbuster had more than 9,000 stores globally (Keane, 2019) and US$5.9 billion in revenue (Harress, 2013) (Exhibit 11).

Netflix (original model)

The Netflix business model was (is) fundamentally different to Blockbuster. Whilst the end result for the consumer was the same, enjoying a movie or television show at home, the means to arrive at that experience reflected a

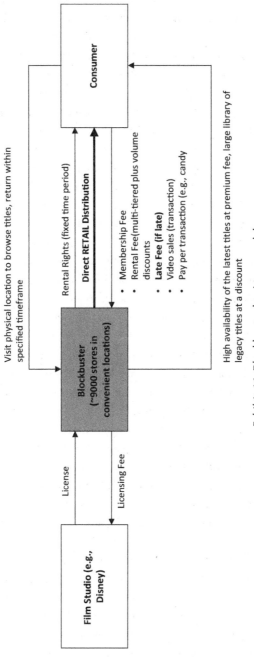

Visit physical location to browse titles, return within specified timeframe

Rental Rights (fixed time period)

Direct RETAIL Distribution

- Membership Fee
- Rental Fee(multi-tiered plus volume discounts
- **Late Fee (if late)**
- Video sales (transaction)
- Pay per transaction (e.g., candy

High availability of the latest titles at premium fee, large library of legacy titles at a discount

License

Licensing Fee

Film Studio (e.g., Disney)

Blockbuster (~9000 stores in convenient locations)

Consumer

Exhibit 11 Blockbuster business model.

different recipe for value creation. The original business model for Netflix was based on the idea that Netflix would offer titles on DVD media via a mail-order subscription (i.e., DVD by mail rentals) for a flat fee per title plus a shipping fee (later abandoned). Titles were typically shipped to the door within 2–3 days from order. This model evolved to a flat fee per month whereby consumers could order a fixed number of titles each month and pay a monthly feel, i.e., a subscription model. Once the videos were viewed by the consumer, they would be returned in the pre-addressed package provided by Netflix, and the next videos selected by the consumers would be shipped. No late fees were levied for videos returned late; however new titles would not be shipped until previous titles were returned. Netflix shared some commonality with Blockbuster (e.g., licence fees paid to content providers) but did not invest in establishing a retail footprint or marketing campaigns, focusing instead on mail order distribution, efficient shipping, and customer word-of-mouth marketing. As such, Netflix had a significantly lower cost structure. The Netflix business model required significantly less scale than Blockbuster, but the model itself was much more scalable. Overall, the key differences lie in the Netflix distribution model and the omission of the late fee, both key threats to the incumbent Blockbuster business model (Exhibit 12).

From the point of view of Blockbuster, the incumbent, the majority of its focus was Y-axis but with a relatively fixed X-axis (i.e., business model). As Netflix challenged Blockbuster (Netflix was the insurgent), its focus was not to compete with Blockbuster by opening up thousands of video stores but rather to challenge Blockbuster by offering a fundamentally different business model and corresponding value proposition. Blockbuster had a lot to lose by changing its business model. For example, as Blockbuster came under pressure from Netflix (and others), it eventually eliminated late fees (effectively a price reduction) and ramped up investment in digital distribution, investing nearly $400 million on these initiatives, but resisted self-cannibalisation making only a half-hearted effort to compete against the Netflix model. This "half pregnant" approach was detrimental to Blockbuster and created unsustainable losses. The elimination of late fees, however, was a poisoned chalice for Blockbuster. While consumers loved it, the incentive to return videos on time disappeared and consumers tended to retain new titles for too long causing supply shortages of new content. When consumers were unable to procure new titles in store, they reduced the frequency of their visits. This vicious cycle cost Blockbuster lost revenue from late fees and repeat purchases. Netflix was an X-axis insurgent competing with a Y-axis incumbent.

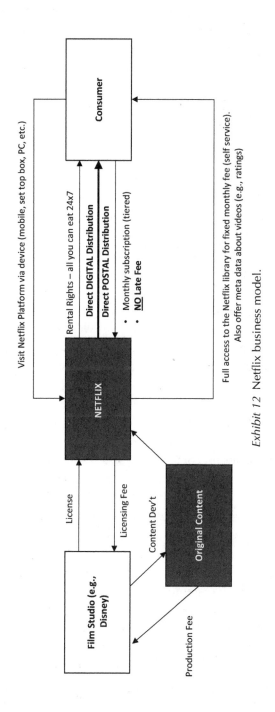

Exhibit 12 Netflix business model.

Blockbuster was not agile enough to adjust its business model and eventually the business collapsed with some 8,999 stores closing, leaving only a single store in operation as of 2019, in Bend Oregon (Keane, 2019)

This need not have happened. Blockbuster's CEO at the time, John Antioco, was aware of the threat represented Netflix and of the fundamental weaknesses of the Blockbuster business model (bricks-and-mortar distribution model and late fees) relative to the Netflix model. Once this threat gathered steam, Blockbuster, led by John Antioco, made an attempt to change its business model by eliminating late fees and ramping up investment in digital distribution but was thwarted by internal resistance, lack of board alignment on the future of the company, and activist investors undermining his efforts in favour of short-term profitability over long-term investment in survival. These efforts to preserve the *status quo* were successful, eventually forcing Antioco to abandon his efforts to transform the business and ultimately costing him his job. Either way, Blockbuster was unable to make the necessary adjustments and eventually exited the market.

Blockbuster's behaviour is consistent with most incumbent competitors. Blockbuster had a model that worked very well, was generating healthy returns, and had a commanding global market share while the context remained stable. The inability of Blockbuster to make X-axis changes to its core business model was both understandable, fatal, and typical. Netflix, by contrast, has made several adjustments to its core business model over the years, even as it has evolved from insurgent to incumbent. Notably, the mail-order rental model was self-cannibalised in favour of video streaming distribution (the elimination of the physical DVD), retaining the monthly subscription model but offering "all-you-can eat" access to titles in its library to consumers available 24×7 online. This required changes in infrastructure and distribution, a change to the subscription model itself, as well as the introduction of numerous new capabilities. Over a relatively short period of time, Netflix refocused its business model to transition the majority of business into digital distribution. As digital distribution reached critical mass and Netflix developed a deep understanding of consumer preferences and behaviour at a very granular level, Netflix again adjusted its business model to focus on development of original content to meet the expanding needs of its customers for content across multiple genres. Netflix, at the time of writing, is now one of the most prolific content houses on the planet spending more than US$12 billion per year on original content (Spangler, 2019) Netflix has become a master of X-axis competition making material changes to its

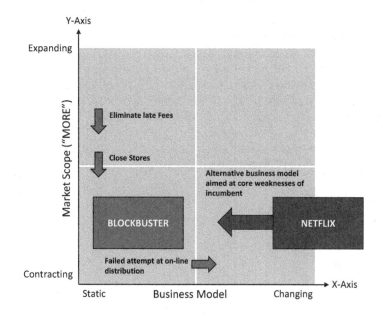

Exhibit 13 Netflix X-axis insurgence.

business model on a regular basis to remain relevant. An X-axis competitor is not encumbered by the perceived need to self-perpetuate its own business model.

The model described in Exhibit 13 shows Netflix attacking on the X-axis by offering the market an alternative business model. This is typical of insurgent disruption. Even though on the screen at home the end product (a film) is largely the same, the models are materially different. We will build on this model in the following chapters.

References

Duca, J, 2010, Housing markets and the financial crisis of 2007–2009: lessons for the future, *Spatial Economic Research Centre*, viewed 18 August 2019, http://eprints. lse.ac.uk/33613/1/sercdp0049.pdf.

Harress, C, 2013, The sad end of Blockbuster Video: the onetime $5 billion company is being liquidated as competition from online giants Netflix and Hulu prove all too much for the iconic brand, *International Business Times*, viewed 16 August 2019, https://ibtimes.com/sad-end-blockbuster-video-onetime-5-billion-compan y-being-liquidated-competition-1496962.

Keane, S, 2019, Blockbuster is down to one location worldwide: the last Australian store ceased rentals on Wednesday, *Cnet*, viewed 18 August 2019, https://cnet.co m/news/blockbuster-is-down-to-one-location-worldwide.

Leopold, T, 2013, Your late fees are waived: Blockbuster closes, *CNN Business*, viewed 16 August 2019, https://edition.cnn.com/2013/11/06/tech/gaming-gadgets/blockbuster-video-stores-impact/index.html.

Osterwalder, A & Pigneur, Y, 2010, *Business Model Generation: A Handbook for Visionaries, Game Changers, and Challengers*. John Wiley & Sons, New Jersey.

Spangler, T, 2019, Netflix spent $12 billion on content in 2018. Analysts expect that to grow to $15 billion this year, *Variety*, viewed 18 August 2019, https://variety.com/2019/digital/news/netflix-content-spending-2019-15-billion-1203112090/.

Strategyzer, 2019, Business model canvas, *Strategyzer*, viewed 18 August 2019, https://strategyzer.com/canvas/business-model-canvas.

7 The Insurgence framework – capability mapping

One of the core elements of every incumbent's strategy is the notion of "core" capability. Core capabilities can be defined as something a firm is *good at* and that has, at one point in its life cycle, provided some competitive advantage. For example, General Electric is great at buying and selling companies, Google is great at search, Amazon is great at supply chain, and so on. Incumbents seek to extrapolate core capabilities by finding new ways of employing these capabilities into new market contexts or to serve unmet customer needs. For example, Coca-Cola, being great at moving around heavy bottles full of liquid soda, found that this capability was amenable to moving around bottled water which is now one of its strongest growth categories. This approach makes a lot of sense. After all, it is much more efficient to exploit existing capabilities than it is to create new ones, particularly if a given capability can be translated into profitable demand.

At the heart of every business model is a set of capabilities. Not all capabilities are created equal, however. A firm may have dozens of capabilities that it employs to deliver value but only a few of these capabilities provide true competitive advantage. For example, payroll processing is an important capability for all firms but not a source of competitive advantage for most (unless a firm is selling payroll services). For a capability to be "core" a firm must be 1) good at it, and 2) it must provide competitive advantage. For our purposes, the term "core" is intended to describe capabilities related to driving the *existing* business model. Many capabilities, while important, are not central to the execution of the business model and are not central to a firm's positioning in the market. Y-axis incumbents will almost always seek to extrapolate their best capabilities in new ways to seek opportunities for growth up the Y-axis. To the extent that there is market capacity for profitable growth driving one or more of the Y-axis variables, the extrapolation of core capabilities can be a source of future performance and competitive advantage. Since the development of capabilities is expensive and time-consuming, it is only natural to seek to maximise the return on a given existing capability in the marketplace.

As firms mature, the efficient operation and execution of existing capabilities becomes more important. Assuming relatively stable market conditions and, importantly, a lack of X-axis competition (i.e., disruption), a firm's capability will reach an equilibrium with the market. In other words, a firm will not build any more capability than is required to deliver its products and services into the market within a given business model. Investment in additional capability will tend to focus on expansion of existing capabilities over development of new ones, particularly as long as opportunities exist to extract additional value from those capabilities along each Y-axis variable (e.g., geographic growth or product line extensions), while holding the X-axis (the business model) constant. We describe the optimisation of these capabilities as "in the box" (see Exhibit 14). Fine-tuning of these capabilities requires significant effort over time to streamline the processes underpinning them, thus improving the productivity and efficiency of each capability. Also required is a mapping of each capability to market needs relative to

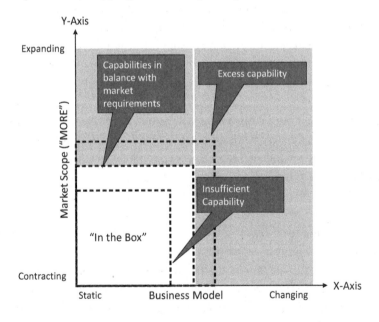

Exhibit 14 In the box.

the competition. This happens simultaneously with investment required to expand these capabilities to meet the market's requirements. A firm that over-builds its capabilities finds the need for periodic restructuring to "right-size" to the market if demand for these capabilities does not materialise. Equally, a firm that underbuilds its capabilities finds it difficult to meet demand and will put stress on the organisation's resources, often to a breaking point. Thus, the inevitable optimisation to find a balance in capability, not too much, not too little. An incumbent firm will seek to achieve this balance and, holding the business model constant, typically will not invest in capabilities that alter the shape of the existing business model, unless a significant threat exists.

Inside-out incumbent firms seeking to drive growth strategies often start with existing "core" capabilities, pushing these capabilities out to new markets and customer segments and finding more and more ways to extract value from each capability. Simultaneously, firms will seek to plug capability gaps where the competition may be stronger or where market dynamics dictate. For example, a firm with strong distribution in the United States or the United Kingdom seeking to access new markets in Indonesia will soon discover that its distribution success in those markets will not readily translate to Indonesian markets and thus will require significant effort or a local partner with the required capability to be successful. The same applies to a tax accounting firm that is great at addressing tax matters for private clients but that is asked by a client to weigh in on corporate tax matters. That firm may find its capabilities lacking on the corporate tax side of the business and will need to develop these further. As a firm grows, choices are made regarding where to deploy resources to enhance its capabilities. One of the Achilles' heels of the incumbent firm is the overemphasis of (i.e., put too much resource and faith in) its existing capabilities, both in terms of competitive advantage and longevity. For example, a historically market-leading taxi company investing in manual, radio dispatchers (a traditional core capability) will find that being the best at this capability was very important 20 years ago, moderately important a decade ago, and is a downright millstone in today's environment. As the context changes, the importance of a given capability also changes.

Some capabilities are so difficult to replicate and so expensive to create that incumbents are well protected over time from traditional competitors let alone insurgents. One example that comes to mind is aircraft wing construction. This capability, particularly with large aircraft, is very complex and requires expensive tooling and the perfect marrying of thousands of critical parts. Wing assembly is very hard to replicate and one of the reasons that the Boeing and Airbus duopoly (fortified incumbents) is so difficult to dislodge. That said, each firm has made costly mistakes in extrapolating existing capabilities. Airbus, misreading the market for jumbo aircraft, made a significant mistake with the development of the A380 (the giant double-decker commercial aircraft), extrapolating decades of capability development into a new platform that failed to find a market large enough to pay back the investment (generally considered a major failure), just as Boeing was pulling back from investing in the ageing 747 platform in favour of smaller and more efficient dual-engine planes focused on point-to-point travel (Garcia, 2019). Boeing, for its part, in an effort to make existing capability platforms more efficient, invested a significant amount of money in the 737 Max program (an extension of a 50+ year-old platform) only to find that they overreached on certain upgrades without properly investing in adequate testing (Leeham News, 2019) and pilot training. In spite of these failures, both firms have been very successful at leveraging their core capabilities to the detriment of their competition to the extent that both Embraer of Brazil and Bombardier of Canada are exiting or have exited the market for single-aisle commercial jets. The default mindset of the incumbent is to erect these capability barriers to such a degree that competition is not able to find a way into the market. We saw this in the Caly's case where the business was able to fend off the national ice cream chains, each time emerging stronger in the market.

Incumbent firms often fall into a "capability trap", whereby the preservation and extension of an existing capability within an existing business model becomes a primary objective for the firm. In unstable market contexts, this becomes a significant risk. The inward focus directed towards discovering new ways to employ existing capability often blinds the firm to the question "what capabilities will propel our *future* competitive advantage?", i.e., distinctive capabilities. This is an important question that seldom gets enough attention in the incumbent firm's strategy-setting process. Even to the extent that the answer is discoverable, the pain and difficulty in nurturing new capabilities (or integrating capabilities purchased on the open market) is significant. In the previous chapter, we saw how Blockbuster was unable, in spite of its efforts, to successfully develop an alternative digital distribution model for getting video content to consumers, instead maintaining focus on existing "core" capabilities until the very end, albeit shrinking this capability back as the market retreated from bricks-and-mortar retail rentals (see Chapter 6, Exhibit 13). As emerging substitutes with different business models and different capabilities gained traction in the market, Blockbuster, holding its business model constant, shrunk down its existing capabilities (including retail footprint, marketing, etc.) until it was no longer sustainable. Blockbuster failed to successfully develop any new capabilities that would provide a new source of competitive advantage, in spite of its early efforts to build an online distribution capability, which were squashed in a bitter internal fight to maintain the *status quo*, cut costs, and stick to the core business. In times of trouble, this is the typical incumbent playbook. The instinct is to "shrink the box" (i.e., cut costs, close stores, etc.) whilst retreating on the Y-axis. This typically involves, initially, doubling down on existing products via promotion or me-too investments (in the Caly's case, we saw the introduction of self-serve in the existing format and in the Blockbuster case we saw the introduction of a no-late-fee policy). Kodak employed the same strategy. Unable to see past its traditional core capability, anchored to the sale and processing of film and the delivery of the "Kodak moment" experience to consumers, Kodak entered the digital age intending to sell and process digital imagery in the very same way as film, in other words, leverage its historical capability investment. In hindsight, we know that these capabilities and the corresponding business model did not translate into the digital world. In the meantime, Kodak's competitors, including FujiXerox, sought new customer problems to solve with new sets of capabilities and have fared rather better than Kodak in the market.

Insurgents approach problems very differently, seeking to constantly develop and build new capabilities while often discarding or diluting existing capabilities in favour of capabilities that will provide the next source of competitive advantage. Capabilities that provide a new source of competitive advantage for a firm can be described as "distinctive capabilities". These firms seek not ways to maintain or extend their old ways of competing but to find new ways of competing via new and distinct capabilities.

Consider McDonald's Australia, a part of the McDonald's global fast-food empire. McDonald's, for much if its history, was a growth company operating a rigidly fixed and highly efficient business model operating at scale with a relentless focus on global uniformity of product and brand (convenient and fast) as well as a highly refined franchising model. In the 2000s McDonald's global growth began to stall, having been focused on geographic growth of new restaurants globally for 40+ years. As the market for new stores became saturated and the competition offering substitute products intensified, McDonald's discovered finding new sources of growth to be very difficult. Y-axis opportunities for growth are limited within the existing

McDonald's business model. While McDonald's has a very successful and scientific approach to new product promotion typically offered "for a limited time only" to reengage existing customers, the resulting growth from these promotions is short term in nature and not particularly sticky. Opportunities to use price as a lever are limited outside of promotions, as the products are already being sold at very close to marginal cost. Though the company has had some success in *lowering* prices to drive up demand (Gasparro, 2017) leveraging its cost position in the market.

McDonald's has a deep and captive relationship with its supply chain and is not prone to deep vertical integration. Traditionally, McDonald's has resisted the urge to seek horizontal adjacencies, instead maintaining focus on the core business and, as such, has some inherent flexibility built into its business model. As a highly efficient operation, focus on refinement of existing core capabilities at McDonald's is legendary. With legions of unskilled workers, the need for McDonald's to standardise processes, such that new and inexperienced workers can be trained and productive in very short order to deliver an accurate and uniform product at scale, is highly important. As such, McDonald's runs a lean operation but has a model that is traditionally inflexible (though incremental improvements in one market are captured and disseminated to all markets if successful). It is hard to imagine a more Y-axis and "in the box" company than McDonald's.

Unlike in the past, the market context for McDonald's is becoming less stable. With more customers demanding healthy food options, green packaging, and vegan and vegetarian menu items and with increasing choice in terms of delivery and product options, McDonald's faces significant pressure to respond to these trends in an increasingly crowded market. Additionally, premium burgers are in demand as a food category and many consumers are increasingly opting for upscale burgers and sides (e.g., truffle fries). Finally, the preferences of consumers, heavily influenced by Amazon's customer-centric business model, are changing towards "give me what I want, when I want it, and how I want it". All of this places McDonald's in a growth pickle (how could I resist the pun?).

For most of its history, McDonald's has focused on a small set of core capabilities:

- Franchising and property management
- Supply chain/supplier management (to enable uniform supply of ingredients at global scale)

- Efficiency of store operations (based on industrial engineering of operations)
- Store management
- Front-line employee training
- Delivery of a uniform customer experience

These capabilities have been finely tuned to McDonald's business context over decades. Historically, McDonald's, like most incumbents, has held its business model relatively constant. In 1993, in Melbourne, Australia, McDonald's departed from this tradition and introduced McCafé to attract consumers seeking convenient but good coffee on par with competitors such as Starbucks. McDonald's, having near ubiquity in terms of urban and suburban locations, was well positioned geographically to offer consumers access to the McCafé offering (focus on coffee and mid-range breakfast bakery items such as muffins, banana bread, etc.). McDonald's, well known for its coffee, was able to stretch its brand in this direction, with most McCafés co-located within traditional restaurants. This was a significant departure for McDonald's and a major success, delivering significant revenue growth on top of a plateauing core business. Since the initial store opening in 1993, McDonald's has expanded the model to select global markets including the United Kingdom and Canada.

McCafé, while mainly a small Y-axis horizontal adjacency with some X-axis characteristics, opened up McDonald's to the value of experimentation in its format and laid the groundwork for the development of new capabilities. In particular, the café experience is different than the traditional McDonald's store experience and requires different training, management, supply chain, etc.

Fast forward to 2014, when McDonald's Australia began experimenting in earnest with other alternative models to drive growth. In light of the above trends (health, environment, premium burgers, customers demanding control) and slow/stagnant growth, McDonald's Australia introduced "Create your Taste", a significant change to its core business model and a major X-axis shift. Create Your Taste involved the introduction of kiosks in the restaurants whereby consumers could enter the restaurant, interact with a giant touchscreen, and configure their own meals with any number of combinations of ingredients (e.g., meat toppings, buns, sides, and drinks). Once configured and paid for at the kiosk, consumers would get a number and the meal would be delivered to the table on a cutting board presented as if in a premium local diner. This was a significant departure for McDonald's. Very quickly, the model was trialled and rolled out to a significant number of stores in Australia throughout 2015 and into 2016.

The launch of Create Your Taste required McDonald's to introduce several new capabilities:

- Customer self-service (via the kiosk)
- App-based ordering and loyalty (i.e., order ahead)
- Tap and go payments
- Data analytics (analysis of customer purchasing behaviour)
- Table service
- Complex (non-standard) order fulfilment

Results were mixed. The introduction of Create Your Taste increased yields in some stores and not in others and required consumers to learn a new way of interaction with a familiar brand and product experience. Average ticket size increased as people configured more expensive burgers reflecting their own preferences. Some of the gains were offset by increased complexity in the kitchen. By all accounts, the average ticket value per transaction increased for Create Your Taste transactions and the model opened up new customer seg-ments (e.g., parents who may have opted not to buy a meal for themselves whilst purchasing meals for their kids were enticed to make purchases, thus opening up Y-axis growth opportunities). Regarding health, an interesting idea is that if McDonald's serves you an unhealthy meal over the counter it's their fault. But if the company gives you total control over the experience, along with healthy options, and you choose to configure an unhealthy meal, that's your fault!

In the end, complexity of the offering and the pushback of some fran-chisees having to purchase new equipment was a challenge. McDonald's dis-continued Create Your Taste in 2017 after running the experiment for almost three years. However, the development of these new capabilities paved the way for McDonald's Australia to alter its model in significant ways, starting with consumer insights (see Exhibit 15). Imagine being able to harvest the data from millions of transactions where people are configuring their own meals with the ability to create an impossibly large number of combinations. In this way, McDonald's begins to look more like Amazon than a fast-food restau-rant. The data analytics capabilities developed from Create Your Taste gave McDonald's enough data to create the most significant alteration to its menu in decades with the introduction of Gourmet Creations, an offering aimed at

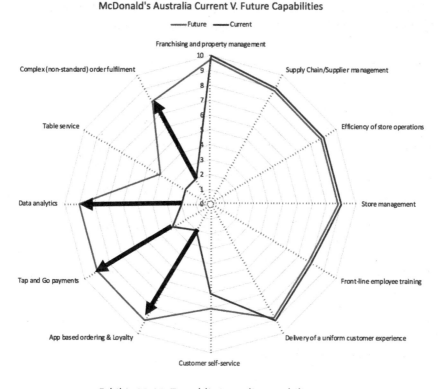

Exhibit 15 McDonald's Australia capability map.

the premium market. Kiosks were repurposed following the Create Your Taste offering to provide a simpler more streamlined experience, albeit with fewer options overall but more relevant choices for consumers including payments (i.e., consumers are still in control of the experience if they want to be but still have access to the counter service if they choose). The rapid decisions to scale and terminate the Create Your Taste model are exciting for an incumbent. Being able to scale an experiment like Create Your Taste, harvest the learnings, and pivot to another significant variation on the business model within two to three years is highly agile and a capability in its own right. These new capabilities are now being expanded to include delivery via Uber Eats and other delivery platforms as well as mobile ordering via the McDonald's app, loyalty, and payments (the kiosk is a transition technology). All of these changes represent a significant modification to the traditional McDonald's business model and capability set and opens up new opportunities on the Y-axis as well as more people engage with the product and brand in new ways.

These changes are paying off. McDonald's after years of stagnant growth is now harvesting the benefits with 20 quarters of period on period growth in Australia and greater than 5% revenue and 13% profit growth globally, well above the Consumer Price Index (CPI) (Brook, 2018).

References

Brook, B, 2018, McDonalds global profits raise due to premium burgers and value menu, *News Pyt Limited*, viewed 19 August 2019, https:.news.com.au/finance/business/retail/mcdonalds-global-profits-rise-due-to-premium-burgers-and-value-menu/news-story/e46fee669ef70f2cd596edb9772c11fc.

Garcia, M, 2019, A jumbo win for Boeing as Airbus announces the end of A380 production, *Forbes*, viewed 26 November 2019, https://forbes.com/sites/marisagarcia/2019/02/14/a-jumbo-win-for-boeing-as-airbus-announces-the-end-of-a380-production/#3cb2757d7460.

Gasparro, A, 2017, McDonald's focus on low prices brings in customers, *The Wall Street Journal*, viewed 19 August 2019, https://wsj.com/articles/mcdonalds-profit-rises-refranchising-drive-dents-revenue-1508851452.

Leeham News and Analysis, 2019, Boeing didn't want to re-engine the 737 but had design standing by, viewed 19 August 2019, https://leehamnews.com/2019/03/20/boeing-didnt-want-to-re-engine-the-737-but-had-design-standing-by/.

8 The Insurgence framework – customer frontier

The role of customers as a source of value for firms cannot be understated. All firms (public, private, not-for-profit included) exist because customers decide (or not) to buy or participate in what the firm offers. While this may seem obvious, in practice it is easy for firms to 'forget' the customer as they grow larger and more complex and graduate to incumbency. Incumbent firms tend to take their customers for granted, pushing their products out to their customers often without adequately understanding their customers' needs or requirements, instead bending to the pressure of meeting their targets, customers be damned. This may seem to be an overstatement, but in my experience it isn't.

The default view of the incumbent is an expectation that customers exist to serve their needs. Customers, after all, sit at the end of the value chain and are the beneficiaries of all the hard work the firm puts in to provide them with products and services. Should customers not be grateful? Once a firm is well established and has a base of customers and an established set of systems and processes to serve those customers, it is not at all unusual for firms to put in the minimum amount of effort required to retain their customers – on the assumption that a quiet customer is a happy customer.

All firms have what we describe as a "customer frontier". This is the interface between the firm and the customer and is illustrated below by the wide arc in Exhibit 16. In practice, the interface exists at all of the touchpoints a company has with its customers and consumers (even if via an intermediary in the case of business to business firms). At the outer edge of the frontier, a firm will find its most demanding and complex customers, those who are willing to buy its most innovative products, provide the most insightful feedback (positive and negative), and, if unsatisfied, move on to other offerings.

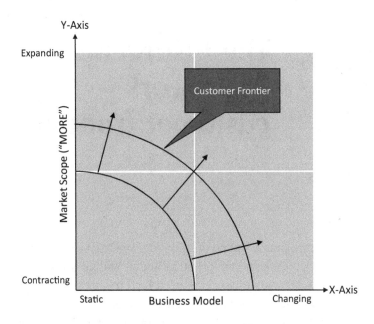

Exhibit 16 Customer frontier.

These customers are not necessarily the most profitable (but often are) and not usually in the majority. As you can see, the customer frontier is shown to overlap the firm's X and Y axes, as customers interact with a firm's products, services, and the business models simultaneously. Over time most customers will retreat away from the firm, looking not only for new features (the domain of the incumbent) on existing products but also new ways to interact with the firm, new experiences, and, increasingly, more control over how they engage with the firm. This is an important point as many firms assume that customer behaviour is relatively fixed, at least in the short to middle term. We observe that customers are moving at an ever-increasing rate away from the status quo offerings provided by incumbents. This applies equally to business to business (B2B), business to consumer (B2C), and business to government (B2G) firms alike.

On the inside of the arc (well inside the "box") are the firm's legacy customers. These customers are not too demanding, do not require much effort to service, and are generally loyal as long as things don't change too much. These customers are quite satisfied with the core stable of products and services offered by the firm and are comfortable operating within the boundaries defined by the established business model. These customers seldom push the firm to innovate and generally represent the silent majority of customers. Between the inner arc and the outer arc are all of the firm's customers at a given time. It is worth noting that this is a generalisation and that different customer segments will position differently along the frontier as customers are not usually homogeneous.

The challenge for all firms is to maintain engagement with their current and target customers as they retreat away from the firm, i.e., stay ahead of the curve (as show by the arrows in Exhibit 16). In a perfectly stable and unchanging world, customers with no other options would retreat away from a firm's offering, model, products, and services at a very slow rate. In a highly unstable world, customers will retreat at a very rapid rate, aggressively seeking alternative offerings, experiences, and business models with which to attract their attentions. Unfortunately for most incumbent firms, customers in general are becoming more demanding and less loyal and thus more likely to at least entertain alternatives even in times of relative stability. Today, customers want far more from their interactions with firms and more say over how and where those interactions transpire, not less. While there are certainly differences in the rate of change in customer behaviour across industry segments, the broad trend is universal. Customers and consumers are programmed to be more demanding and fickler and will switch if a better offer is available. Customers also increasingly value more than the traditional price, service, and convenience propositions and increasingly seek experiences, alignment to their values (e.g., sustainable sourcing), and a voice in how a firm engages with them. In short, across the board, customers are redefining their engagement with firms actively whereas historically they were, by and large, passive.

Insurgents tend to exploit the weakness of incumbents at the frontier of the incumbent's customer relationships by offering a materially different experience, value proposition, and business model (or engagement model from the customer's point of view). Ripe for the picking, these customers will typically fall into one of four categories: 1) bored and fickle, 2) unconsciously unsatisfied, 3) consciously unsatisfied, and 4) satisfied but curious and open to alternatives.

The rise of Xero, an accounting software provider established in 2006 in New Zealand to service the small- to medium-enterprise market up against MYOB, the incumbent market leader, illustrates this point very well. Xero recognised that MYOB was underserving its customers with a clumsy and non-intuitive desktop-based user interface and an outdated business model not reflective of the future of applications (i.e., cloud-based SAAS business model, universal ledger, intuitive user interface, etc.) and entered the market as a listed insurgent to disrupt MYOB. MYOB, the market-leading incumbent (outside the United States), was caught unawares and lost significant market share to Xero as customers defected to the new model, Xero now leading MYOB in several key markets (Newsroom.co.nz, 2018).

Many of these customers were "satisfied enough" with MYOB but in spite of relatively high switching costs opted to take the risk and adopt the Xero solution. Xero was able to simultaneously exploit MYOB's weaknesses on both the Y and X axes by offering a more intuitive product and a more flexible cloud-based engagement model for its customers. Early adopters of Xero were, according to Morgan Stanley, "more progressive and agile firms" (Tadros and Redrup, 2018). MYOB, slow to adapt to this change, has invested aggressively to balance the scales back in its favour but is playing catch up. It always pays to look for lazy competitors and unconsciously unsatisfied customers when seeking to disrupt a competitor.

Incumbents tend to, over time, expect customers to fall into, and stay in, the firm's orbit (see Exhibit 17). Incumbents create barriers for customers to remain "sticky" (recall the example of my photos on the Apple platform). In doing so, incumbents make the broad assumption that customers will always continue to want to: 1) buy their products and engage with their value propositions (e.g., film, taxis, etc.), 2) that customers are largely passive and once engaged stay engaged, 3) that customers exist to serve the firm and not the other way around, and 4) that the firm need only provide adequate engagement at existing touchpoints to maintain relevance to customers. In the "firm centric" view of the incumbent, customers are the commodity. In this planetary model, customers are generally viewed as well outside of the firm and engaged mainly through existing touchpoints and measured via traditional market research

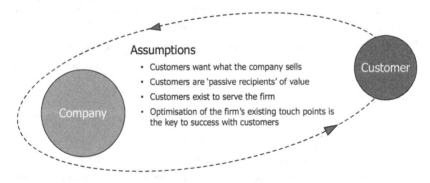

Exhibit 17 Customer orbiting the company.

and satisfaction surveys, and, more recently, Net Promoter Score (NPS) (see below). As such customers are viewed as outside of the firm's boundaries to be engaged only on terms dictated by the firm and not the customer. The *status quo* is thus rigorously defended, and customers are encouraged to only accept change offered or initiated by the firm. Of course, customers are always free to vote with their feet, but over time this firm-centric approach leads consumers to build up a sort of potential energy in their interactions with the firm (i.e., "I'll stay only until something better comes along") which can become dynamic and kinetic at a very rapid rate as shown above in the Xero case.

The take-up of Uber/Lyft/Grab vs. the incumbent taxi model is a great example. Customers grudgingly accept an inferior offering from incumbent taxi providers, each time building negative goodwill until an alternative arises that fundamentally alters their perspective (superior offering, different engagement model, an opportunity to participate via direct feedback, etc.) on what the experience should look like.

Insurgents tend to be what we describe as "customer proximate". By necessity, insurgent firms must orbit the customers and bring them into the tent along the way (see Exhibit 18). Customer-proximate firms recognise that the power and control are increasingly in the hands of the customers and find ways to enable prospective customers to exercise this power via mechanisms of engagement (e.g., engagement platforms), providing opportunities for customers to directly participate in how value is created (e.g., solution design, experience design, etc.) and build their processes around the needs of customers rather than expect customers to map to existing processes. Admittedly, once processes are created, implemented and then scaled up it becomes more difficult to alter these processes as customers inevitably retreat away from the firm, thus the gravity towards incumbency over time.

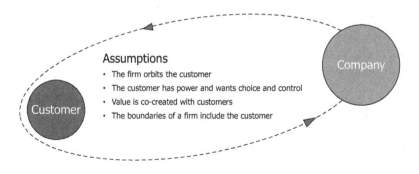

Assumptions
- The firm orbits the customer
- The customer has power and wants choice and control
- Value is co-created with customers
- The boundaries of a firm include the customer

Customer

Company

Exhibit 18 Company orbiting the customer.

Finally, the boundaries of the customer-proximate firm extend to include customers in the tent not outside it. This is an important point. For example, in 25 years of working with companies across most industries and on six continents, I have rarely, if ever, seen customers directly represented in an incumbent's strategy making or product development processes, yet this is almost always the case for insurgents.

Incumbent firms are waking up to the idea of customers as a key priority and many, even most, firms recognise now that customers are more important than ever. It is now common to see a flurry of activity in an incumbent's marketing function to create journey maps representing the customer's journey and highlighting the many touchpoints the firm has with a customer. Many firms now also employ NPS to better understand how engaged customers are with the firm (NPS is roughly defined as the percentage of supporters minus the percentage of detractors based on the question "how likely are you (the customer) to recommend us (the firm)" on a scale of 1–10, 10 being the highest). However, even these tools are, for the most part, company-, not customer-centric. Journey maps, for example, often fall short of their potential by prioritising "pain points" at existing touchpoints rather than imagining new opportunities for interacting with customers (i.e., discovery of new touchpoints). NPS, while very helpful as a metric, is still mostly about the firm ("how likely are YOU to recommend US", emphasis on the "US"), not the customer. These are excellent tools but fall short of their potential to help firms become more customer-proximate.

The journey towards customer proximity is a difficult one for incumbents precisely because they tend to optimise from the inside-out not the outside-in. Insurgents find the path easier, not being encumbered by the many constraints experienced by incumbents as well as the absolute necessity of being as close to customers as possible. Insurgents have more degrees of freedom, particularly in early stages of maturity, to build around the customer's wants and needs and can, often, thus leapfrog incumbents at a rapid rate as we saw with Xero and MYOB above.

There are typically five stages that a firm goes through on the path to customer proximity. These are described below.

Stage 1: product centric

Product-centric firms view customers primarily as a means to an end and tend to be very self-centred in their interactions with customers. Their overwhelming belief in the superiority of their products or services and arrogance built on past successes dominate their mindset. Product-centric firms know what's best for their customers and look to push their solutions out to the market seeking passive customers that are willing to buy their products or services, no questions asked, "thank you very much". These companies prioritise their own internal metrics over customer metrics, seeking to improve product penetration and market share regardless of customer satisfaction or engagement. Product centricity is the domain of the incumbent, often imbued with monopolistic or oligopolistic positioning in tightly regulated markets (e.g., utilities, phone companies, banks, taxis, etc.). These firms tend not to invest a significant amount of effort in building customer equity but invest heavily in new features and benefits of existing products to push out to customers. At this stage of development, the customer is both "outside the tent" and relatively powerless to influence the firm's direction. Customers' basic needs are met to an "acceptable" standard. Consequently, product-centric firms can only exist in stable and relatively protected environments. When you are in your economy airline seat and your not so friendly flight attendant acts as if your request for a cup of water is the greatest imposition in the history of mankind, you are experiencing a product-centric firm and being treated as a captive customer with few options, having already made the decision to purchase the product. My telephone company is product-centric. Whenever I have a problem (usually because of being overcharged for service I did not receive), I have to allocate up to a half-day of my time to get the problem resolved, often bouncing from one customer service representative to another, each time having to re-explain the problem until, finally, I receive assurances by the company that the problem will be resolved. The problem almost never is resolved and, reluctantly, I accept the overcharging because my time (and mental health) is more important to me. Unfortunately, there are few switching options and I am captive as a customer. As soon as a viable alternative comes along, I'm gone. I'm consciously unsatisfied.

Stage 2: service oriented

Inevitably, competition drives product-centric firms towards a service orientation whereby the firm "discovers" that they have customers, typically owing to a critical mass of customer complaints, ombudsman cases, and low satisfaction. Service-oriented firms realise that there is a need to resolve customer complaints efficiently to maintain their brand positioning and hold onto existing customers. As such, the investment in customer service to resolve complaints and customer problems becomes an important priority. These firms seek to solve customer's immediate problems with products and service whilst still prioritising their own internal focus, coldly calculating the costs and benefits of providing good customer service. As they develop, service-oriented firms become very efficient at handling complaints and resolving customer problems, building some goodwill in the process, i.e., "the flight was late but at least the flight attendant was willing to give me a glass of water *and* I got a discount voucher for my next flight". Service-oriented firms realise the necessity of keeping customers "not unsatisfied" lest they defect to competitors or spend less money with them. As it is cheaper in the long run to keep customers happy than it is to lose them, these firms invest heavily in training front-line staff and systems to handle complaints and resolve satisfaction issues, whilst upselling and cross-selling their products. Service orientation, while commendable, is a relatively low bar for firms in times of turbulent change and serves well as an incumbent approach to retaining customers in the box (i.e., not at the frontier). American Express comes to mind as a particularly good service-oriented firm. I once had my AMEX card stolen after hours on a business trip to Bahrain and they managed to have a new card at my hotel the very next morning without any hassle, which saved me a lot of headache.

Stage 3: customer centricity

Customer centricity has gathered a lot of momentum in recent years as incumbent firms realise that the relationship they have with their customers is both important in its own right but also a key source of competitive advantage. Customer-centric firms break the "product first" mindset and are often able to prioritise customers ahead of their own needs (e.g., products), understanding intuitively that bringing joy to customers is a key driver of loyalty and repeat purchase as well as brand equity. These firms work hard to build a superior experience at every touchpoint with customers, resolving issues for customers in real time and empowering front-line staff to make decisions on behalf of the customer. My father, once a mid-level executive at Kodak, had a few simple rules for his customer-facing teams that always resonated with me: 1) if it's good for the customer and the company, "do it and don't ask anyone for permission"; 2) if it's good for the customer but not the company, "you are empowered to do what it takes to help the customer and we will sort it out after the fact"; and 3) if it's bad for the customer and the company, well then "don't do it". I recollect that he had some difficulties at times providing internal air cover for employees on #2 and spent a lot of time training employees what "good" looks like for both the company and the customer. Customer-centric companies measure customer satisfaction and NPS and pay particular attention to these metrics in their performance management processes. Above all, customer-centric firms are masters of rule #2. The customer breaks all ties. For example, Amazon will allow you to return an audiobook, no questions asked, for any reason whatsoever if you didn't like the title, the narrator, or the story and receive another book at no charge. Businessdictionary.com defines customer centricity as "creating a positive consumer experience at the point-of-sale and post-sale" (*Business Dictionary*, 2019). This definition recognises the importance of "experience" in the interaction with customers throughout the lifecycle of the relationship with the customer, as related primarily to the transaction between the company and the customer. Customer centricity requires a high degree of focus on employee satisfaction and engagement. Unhappy or exploited workers will not represent the company well to their customers. Company rhetoric, "we are customer centric", is not authentic unless customer-facing employees are genuine about delighting their customers. Firms that expect customer-centric behaviour from their employees but cheat on training, employee pay, and incentives, and, importantly, punish, rather than reward #2 behaviours, face the risk of slipping backwards to the service orientation stage of development. The rewards that customer-centric companies seek are primarily lifetime value and loyalty derived from good customer relationships. Customer centricity represents a waypoint on the path to customer proximity but falls short of achieving the "firm orbiting the customer" and is more about meeting the customer on even terms. For many firms, this may be sufficient, particularly where incumbent competition is lazy and insurgent competition is not yet active.

I recently came across a company facing a customer centricity dilemma. The firm, amid a major drive to espouse customer centricity across the business (a transportation company), was struggling with the paradox of providing greater customer empowerment through the introduction of self-service options for customers, while facing a backlash from employees knowing full well that many front-line jobs were at risk of being made redundant. To address this, the firm created an "inverted management philosophy", whereby all roles from the CEO down and across the business were challenged to find new ways to support front-line staff, identify opportunities to create new roles to serve the customer, and help customers make the transition to the self-service environment. Front-line staff were given "a seat at the table" to help discover new ways to serve customer needs and build new roles to make this possible. One insight that came from this process was a recognition that employees spend time (and therefore money) on disabling certain functionality for some customers being offered a lower-tier product selection. In other words, the company was *spending more money* to diminish the customer experience by de-specifying the product. Put another way, the lower-tier product was more expensive to deliver than the higher-tier product whilst at the same time delivering an inferior customer experience. This practice was abolished on the spot by management once the policy was framed against the customer centricity principal. In this case, an engaged employee, potentially acting against her own best interests (she was part of the team disabling the functionality), acted for the customer because she trusted management to reward her behaviour. She is now managing the customer training programme for the transition to self-service, having been promoted to this role for her commitment to the principle of customer centricity.

Stage 4: co-creation

Over the last 15 years, I was fortunate to have the opportunity to work closely with Professor Venkat Ramaswamy, of the University of Michigan, as he and several of his colleagues developed their thinking and published several books on the topic of co-creation (Ramaswamy and Gouillart, 2010). A key learning from this experience, and from working with our clients over this time, is that the boundary of a firm is largely artificial. As tribal beings, we tend to create "constraints of the mind" for want of membership on a team, in an organisation, or as part of a functional group (e.g., the marketing team). Stage 4 firms transcend these constraints and fundamentally recognise the importance of deep involvement and engagement of customers at the frontier I described above (see Exhibit 16). They expand the boundaries of the firm such that the customer (and other stakeholders) can participate in, and contribute to, value creation (on both the supply and demand side), both inside the firm and across the chain of experiences from the perspective of the customer. These firms prioritise co-design with customers to create mutually beneficial value creation, i.e., "the customer wins and we win". In short, co-creation is a way of thinking that allows firms and customers alike to discover and harness each other's perspectives to find new opportunities for value creation. This often results in the development of new products and business models at the frontier of interactions between companies and customers (and other stakeholders).

For incumbents, co-creation is difficult because it requires the suspension of the traditional control mentality in favour of "mutually beneficial engagement" with customers to discover new territory to create value. A truly co-creative firm will create platforms that help customers interact not only with the firm in new and different ways but also with their own networks of stakeholders, often independent of the company. Additionally, ongoing co-creation will be embedded in the firm's business model such that the customers take ownership of some part of the value creation for both their own benefit and for the firm. Companies such as Starbucks, Nike, IKEA, LEGO, and DeWalt have fundamentally changed the way they run part or all of their businesses to harness co-creation with customers. Stage 4 companies look for opportunities to embed customers deeply into their business models and help customers find new ways to engage with the world around them, often even with competitors. These companies prioritise the experiences on all sides of each interaction. For example, Nike, an incumbent shoe manufacturer and marketer, evolved Nike+ from a discovery that the realm of an athlete's (runner) experiences extend well beyond the "in-store purchasing" experience (a consumer might purchase shoes only two to three times per year). These other experiences, including "listening to music while running" and "route planning", were, from the consumer's perspective, very important but essentially opaque to Nike. Through co-creation, Nike was able to build a platform, Nike+, with Apple as key partner to offer a solution at scale to help customers enhance their running experience, initially linking an iPod, the shoe, and the resulting data together to fuel the experience and eventually creating an integrated experience embedded into the Apple Watch and the Nike+ App (Ramaswamy, 2008). The customers win because they have a better overall experience (well beyond the shoe) and Nike wins because they can create a meaningful connection with consumers in an area that 1) is important to consumers and 2) provides insight into consumer behaviour that cannot be gleaned from traditional market research.

87

Stage 5: customer proximity

The fifth and final stage is customer proximity (see Exhibit 19). Customer proximity is achieved when a firm is finally able to orbit the customer and the business itself is so close to the customer or consumer so as to be symbiotic (i.e., essential to both parties). Few incumbent firms are able to achieve this level of commitment to customers, yet most insurgent firms are customer proximate by design. Only as complexity and functionalisation grows do insurgent firms, if they are not paying attention, lose their grip. The progression through each of the above stages towards customer proximity is cumulative and brings forward the best of each stage before it. We have identified nine key attributes to describe a customer-proximate firm. Few firms will exhibit all nine of these attributes at all times.

1. **Proximity:** Proximity is a measure of how close the firm is to the customer. In other words, what percentage of roles in the firm have meaningful customer contact in a given time period. Note the "meaningful" distinction is not about contact related to problems created by the firm (i.e., failure demand)! To illustrate, as part of a Royal Commission investigating the Australian Banking industry in 2018, Shayne Elliott, then CEO of ANZ Bank, one of Australia's "big 4" banks, made a public comment that less than 20% of the more than 50,000 employees ever see a

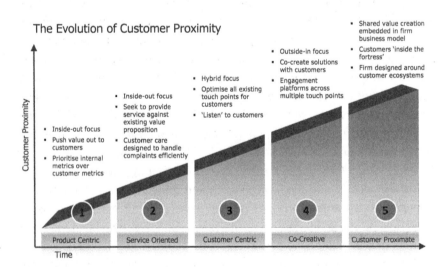

Exhibit 19 Customer proximity evolution.

customer and that the result is a firm that is overly focused on shareholders and internal stakeholders relative to customers and the community (ABC News, 2018). We would describe this as a low degree of customer proximity, typical of incumbents. There is no "perfect ratio" for proximity. However, we believe that firms that drop below about 60% should be concerned. Naturally, this varies by industry, for a consulting firm the lower limit might be 90% and for an online retailer the lower limit might be 25%. What percentage of your company's roles have meaningful customer contact?

2. **Co-creativity:** Co-creativity refers to the degree to which the customer is a participant in value creation in your firm. For example, at IKEA, the customer is directly involved in the final step of production (final assembly) for many of their products. The business model itself brings the customer into the manufacturing process. This is co-creativity. Customer self-service in a supermarket is another example of co-creativity. Some may argue that this creates a distance between the company and the customer in a traditional human contact sense. However, by giving the customer an opportunity to take ownership of part of the value-creation process presents new opportunities for engagement. For example, the self-service software can collect meaningful data about customer service and the new role created whereby in-store staff greets every customer going through the self-serve queue can create additional opportunities for engagement. Meanwhile, the customer wins by saving time he or she would have otherwise spent waiting in the queue. Co-creativity is a Stage 4 attribute that carries forward to Stage 5.

3. **Co-creation:** In this context, we refer to co-creation as "the customer has a seat at the table". For example, to what degree do customers contribute insight into the company decision processes: what products to offer, company strategy, service design, etc. Customer-proximate firms bring customers inside the tent and look for opportunities to expand the traditional one-way dialogue with customers where the firm guides the conversations and asks the questions to one of open contact with customers where the customer can provide meaningful insight into how the company can co-create value on their terms. This approach is particularly effective for B2B firms seeking to build deeper relationships with their customers. Only through frequent, open, and meaningful dialogue with customers can frontier opportunities be discovered. Traditional customer surveys and marketing research techniques often fail to deliver

meaningful insights precisely because the company does not know what questions to ask. Incumbents ask, "What do you think about this new product, do you like it?" Insurgents ask, "What are we solving for together and how can we combine our resources to create a solution?" This kind of contact is especially necessary for "frontier" customers and less interesting for "legacy" customers. Insurgents undermine incumbents by changing the conversation with customers and thus discovering their real needs unencumbered by the "we can't do that" baggage incumbents bring to the party.

4. **Touchpoints:** A customer-proximate firm places emphasis on discovering and forging new touchpoints with customers that transcend traditional touchpoints (e.g., point of sale) where the customer experience is well known. While it is important, and often low-hanging fruit, to improve the experience at existing touchpoints, the value tends to be very incremental. Journey mapping can be a useful tool to help discover new touchpoints but only if the exercise is fundamentally carried out from the viewpoint of the customer and the customer's network of stakeholders. From our experience, most journey mapping efforts that do not embrace this philosophy yield little benefit other than process improvement and resolution of existing "pain points" customers have at known touchpoints.

5. **Peer-peer:** For the most part, peer-peer interactions between customers and their stakeholders are invisible to the firm. Incumbents, in particular, are usually uncomfortable connecting customers for fear of losing control of the conversation or receiving negative feedback. Today, much of this conversation occurs on social media platforms where customers share information with each other about their experiences with your products and services. Most companies are aware of this "chatter" and monitor it to keep abreast of trending information that could pose a risk (or opportunity) for the firm. However, few incumbent firms encourage and enable customers to engage in the background, independent of the company. For example, frontier customers will often share use case "hacks" regarding the use of your products with each other to solve specific problems not on the "approved use" list. Customer-proximate firms proactively provide these opportunities for customers (and their friends, families, partners, etc.) to engage with each other either online or face to face. As an example, a bank enabling its customers to lend each other money for microloans. What bank in their right mind would allow this? Usually not the incumbent bank.

6. **Measurement:** It is well known that measurement drives behaviour in a firm. Few mainstream metrics for Stage 4 and Stage 5 companies exist. As mentioned above, NPS and customer satisfaction and complaints ratings are the predominant metrics for firms to evaluate and reward customer interaction but these are company-centric and insufficient, in their own right, to adequately measure customer proximity. This is an area that requires more work as most metrics in general use are insufficient to measure customer proximity. Here are a few starters:

   a. Customer proximity: Percentage of roles with meaningful customer contact (i.e., contact that adds value with customers vs. resolving problems created by the company)
   b. Customer proximity composite score: Customer rating of the firm on the nine attributes of customer proximity (scale 1–10)
   c. Customer openness: Percentage company processes open to customer co-creation
   d. Customer relevance: Percentage mapping of firm to *customer* processes (i.e., what percentage of possible touchpoints does the company engage with customers in)

   We welcome feedback on how your firm, incumbent or insurgent, measures your proximity to customers.
7. **Culture:** Above all other factors, customer proximity requires a culture that embraces the notion of the firm orbiting the customer. Customer-proximate firms are deeply committed to building a culture that embraces customers as "part of the team". In these firms, "the customer wins all ties" is deeply embedded in the psyche of all of the firm's people. Leadership takes a stand to side with the customer whenever possible and empowers employees to make snap decisions at the front line to support customer's needs. For example, Zappos, a once-insurgent online shoe retailer (now owned by Amazon), famously directed customers to competitor websites if they were unable to provide items for them due to stock-out or lack of product availability (Pondefract, 2015). This level of customer proximity creates tremendous customer loyalty. Further, the leadership in the organisation recognises their role in supporting customer-facing staff to be successful, enabled, and empowered.
8. **Advocacy:** A customer-proximate firm has legions of advocates at a high level of engagement. Advocacy is well covered by NPS in terms of

measurement, but in practice for most incumbent firms, the NPS data does not translate into action for those advocates in terms of harnessing the advocates as *active* ambassadors or contributors to a firm's mission. Customer-proximate firms also develop internal customer advocates, in other words, people inside the firm who advocate for the customer to help the firm make decisions that add value to the customer. Many firms don't go beyond knowing that they have advocates and adding to their number (collecting). Providing opportunities for advocates to participate can also be a significant source of untapped resource beyond seeking referrals for new business. One education client we worked with felt constrained in the execution of their strategy owing to a perceived resource constraint. When asked how many engaged advocates in the recently graduated student pool, they proudly announced that more than 25% of their former students (in the last 3 years) were "engaged advocates" (i.e., had high NPS). After identifying that this group was a significant potential resource pool that could contribute in many ways to reduce the resource constraint, a programme was created to bring student and alumni volunteers into the organisation to help with recruiting, applications design, course design, and post-graduation placement (employment). In exchange for real-world experience, the firm was able to bridge the resource gap while simultaneously increasing its pool of advocates as the word got out.

9. **Narrative:** Much has been written in recent years about the value of storytelling in the corporate environment. This too applies to what we describe as stories of customer heroics. Customer-proximate firms create a mythology around incredible stories of "over the top" efforts for customers. One story I recall hearing more than 25 years ago, possibly apocryphal, was a story of a Federal Express employee in Memphis who drove overnight in a snowstorm from Memphis to Colorado to deliver a wedding dress to a bride who needed it the next day. As the delivery plane was not able to fly, the employee, on his own initiative, took it upon himself to make the trip and managed to get the dress there on time. A similar story appeared in 2017 when another FedEx employee saved a San Diego bride's big day in similar, albeit less dramatic, fashion (Schwartz, 2017). FedEx celebrates and enshrines these stories and is so famous for their devotion to helping customers that the movie Castaway, with Tom Hanks playing a FedEx employee stranded on a desert island, had a subplot relating to the eventual

delivery of a package years later when the protagonist returned home (IMDb, 2000).

Truly customer-proximate firms are quite rare, and many firms aspire to lead their industries on this score. Small and nimble insurgents, unencumbered by weighty policies and procedures, legal teams, etc., are more able to orbit customers than incumbents and become customer-proximate. However, customer proximity is a choice for incumbents to make, or not. As market conditions become less stable for a firm and customers retreat faster and further away from the firm's offering and model, customer proximity is an essential ingredient to insurgence. As a rule, the further a company is from its customers, the more vulnerable that firm is to disruption when the change comes.

References

ABC News, 2018, Banking royal commission: ANZ chief says many employees 'dehumanise' work as 'they don't see a customer', *ABC News*, viewed 19 August 2019, https://.abc.net.au/news/2018-06-30/anz-chief-says-bank-employees-dehumanise-work-dont-see-customer/9927340.

Business Dictionary, 2019, viewed 19 August 2019, http://www.businessdictionary.com/definition/customer-centric.html.

IMBd, 2000, *Cast Away* Plot, viewed 19 August 2019, https://imdb.com/title/tt0162222/plotsummary.

Newsroom.co.nz, 2018, MYOB and Xero fight for market share, viewed 19 August 2019, https://newsroom.co.nz/2018/11/16/324508/myob-celebrates-accelerating-growth.

Pontefract, D, 2015, What is happening at Zappos?, *Forbes*, viewed 18 August 2019, https://forbes.com/sites/danpontefract/2015/05/11/what-is-happening-at-zappos/#7cf304e24ed8.

Ramaswamy, V, 2008, Co-creating value through customers' experiences: the Nike case, *Strategy & Leadership*, vol. 36, no. 5, pp. 9–14, Emerald Group Publishing Limited, viewed 18 August 2019, http://icesi.edu.co/blogs/bitacorainnovacion141/files/2014/04/1742554.pdf.

Ramaswamy, V & Gouillart, F, 2010, Building the co-operative enterprise, *Harvard Business Review*, https://hbr.org/2010/10/building-the-co-creative-enterprise.

Schwartz, P, 2017, Rialto Fedx employee saves a bride's big day, *The Press – Enterprise*, viewed 19 August 19, https://pe.com/2017/05/04/rialto-fedex-employee-saves-a-brides-big-day/.

Tadros, E & Redrup, Y, 2018, Xero-only firms a challenge for MYOP, *Financial Review*, viewed 09 October 2018, https://afr.com/technology/xeroonly-firms-a-challenge-for-myob-20181009-h16en8.

9 | The Insurgence framework – trend mapping

One of the most vexing questions an incumbent must face relates to the stability of the market, i.e., how stable is your competitive environment and at what point does instability critically undermine a firm's competitive position? We saw in both the Caly's and Blockbuster cases how quickly instability can fatally undermine a firm's business model and, by contrast, a long unwinding of the model in the case of Kodak. Understanding and predicting trends is as much an art as it is a science for most firms. Trends, like bubbles on the surface of a stream, tend to roll along slowly at first combining one after another until they burst, creating ripples that propagate downstream. Most firms keep a watching brief on key trends over time but are notoriously poor at understanding how and when these trends will converge to drive change at scale.

The annual strategy process in most middle-large incumbent firms is often particularly unsuited to help these firms predict the future for several reasons. First, these firms don't want things to change too much and, as such, tend to suffer from confirmation bias, discounting important trends as favourable. (In the Caly's case – self-serve frozen yogurt, great, we can do that too!) Second, the tools employed in most strategy processes are insufficient to adequately draw insights for an incumbent in turbulent times. Finally, not enough time is set aside for deep thinking on how evolving trends will reshape the business context, primarily because running the existing business is so damn time-consuming. The result is often lazy and biased thinking that tends not to deliver any insights beyond the obvious and well known.

On the second point, by far the most widely used trend analysis tools are SWOT (strengths, weaknesses, opportunities, and threats) and PESTEL (political, environmental, social, technology, economic, legal). These tools have the benefit of being easy to use and understand but, like many "paint by numbers" approaches, fall down in the implementation and insight harvesting. In the typical strategy process, templates are created to capture the SWOT and PESTEL analysis and distributed to business unit managers to "fill out". Busy business unit managers, already stretched to meet year-end targets, either assign these to junior staff, consultants, or fill them in on the weekend or on the way to the annual strategy retreat (some of you are laughing here, I've been there too). These tools typically provide very little insight when the context is relatively stable, producing only "known" insights, and even less insight when instability reigns. Imagine getting a PESTEL template with instructions to identify trends that might have a future impact on your firm. Naturally, you would start with the P (political) and identify several of these trends (e.g., looming change of government) and work your way to the L (it's 2 am and you're exhausted by now). You declare victory having surfaced 18 trends! Why 18? Given a template with six boxes, you might appear lazy only filling in one trend per box! The same applies to your SWOT analysis. While this is a bit of tongue-in-cheek, it accurately describes how many businesses develop and analyse trends. My point is that these tools, while helpful in stable environments, perhaps to validate what you are doing or to make incremental changes, are of limited value when disruption is on the horizon.

More sophisticated incumbent businesses apply scenario planning to bring the PESTEL trends to life, using these trends to create "alternative futures" (usually four) to determine what the environmental context might look like at a defined point in the future, say 5 years. The main idea then is to develop strategies that are robust to more than one or all of the alternative futures. This is a more useful method, but also more time-consuming, for the firm to discover each alternative future and what is required to adapt to those futures. Typically, once these alternative futures are discovered, a process takes place whereby the leadership rationalises their current strategy/actions/ activity as "future proof" with a watching brief on certain trends. Overall, scenario planning is better than the above described SWOT/PESTEL templating process and is often used in concert with these techniques. The main drawback of scenario planning is that it usually does not adequately factor in how customers, competitors (obvious and otherwise), and other stakeholders might respond to the most relevant trends (see below).

Insurgents don't suffer from these constraints of the mind. They are self-programmed to deeply understand and exploit (even drive) certain trends at the expense of the reigning incumbents and work hard to discover when certain trends will converge together to form a "tipping point". The insurgent process is more biased towards deep thinking and, generally, more organic and less methodology-driven. Initially at least, insurgents don't need a very large market, as compared to the incumbent(s), and can thus focus attention on the early adoption/emergence of certain trends and, hopefully, survive until the most critical trends converge allowing their business model to reach scale. As once stated by writer William Gibson, "The future is already here – it is just not very evenly distributed". Opposite to incumbents, insurgents tend to overvalue the timing and impact of certain trends, sometimes coming out of the gate too soon, thus waiting for the market to sufficiently mature.

The frame of the incumbent is different from the insurgent. The incumbent's mindset is to preserve and extend, whereas the insurgent mindset is to disrupt and displace. This means that each, by definition, will be solving for something fundamentally different. "What are you solving for?" is a powerful question by itself, made more powerful by understanding what your competitors, customers, and other stakeholders are solving for. For incumbents, the tendency is to project their own desired future ("more") onto the competition (i.e., assume that all players want the same thing), and for insurgents, the goal is to solve for something very different from the incumbents (i.e., an objective function that may appear irrational or even outright crazy to the incumbents).

For example, a former insurance client had a core product that generated 60% of its revenue and 65% of its profit. This product was on offer for 75 years and had a loyal following amongst its customers. The product generated >60% gross margins. There were, over most of the last 25 years, only two competitors in the market offering a similar product, with, by all accounts, a very similar cost and margin structure. Their initial scan of market trends was heavily focused on the market as-is with the usual SWOT/PESTEL analysis employed to seek insight about how the industry might evolve over time. The analysis did not include any insights about emerging customers and changing customer behaviours. One emerging competitor we discovered outside this process was a supermarket chain that was positioning itself to offer similar insurance at a *price* roughly equivalent to the *cost* of the insurance provider. Management discounted this competitor outright on the basis that they assumed that the emerging competitor could not make money on the product and would thus exit the market in due course. As such, the competitor did not feature in their thinking and this class of emerging competition was not flagged as a threat. An objective observer would disagree. The supermarket chain was willing to offer this product at break-even in order to drive loyalty and traffic to support its core business selling groceries. For the insurance company, this was a potentially significant threat as the product represented 65% of the firm's profit and competing at marginal cost would have been economic suicide. Their projection of their own assumptions (make money) onto what the competition was solving for (loyalty and traffic) was a potentially fatal mistake. Fortunately, the insurance company was able to reframe their perspective and address the threat by innovating the product and the business model, thus disrupting their own offering and eventually forcing the new competition into a narrow niche. It is essential for management to understand not just *what* new or emerging competition might do but also to understand deeply the why. Incumbents are particularly poor at this kind of empathy and must work hard to develop these perspectives.

The following is a case study using Ford Motor Company and Tesla to develop this point. It is worth pointing out that this case is written from an outsider's perspective and may not be fully accurate in all details. As such, it is presented as illustrative and I make apologies in advance for any inaccuracies.

In May of 2017, Mark Fields', chief executive Officer at Ford Motor Company, tenure ended and he was replaced by Jim Hackett, formerly of Steelcase and the University of Michigan. Fields' removal was due to a combination of factors, including declining share price (down ~35% over his 3-year tenure), a miscalculation related to a plant relocation announcement to Mexico during the 2016 presidential campaign (then candidate Donald Trump picked Fields as a poster boy for the outsourcing of American jobs at the time), but mostly because his actions did not match up to his rhetoric around the evolution of Ford to the future of transportation including "smart mobility" (electric and autonomous vehicles). In short, the board perceived Ford, under Mark Fields (Felton, 2017), as moving too slowly (or at least slower than the competition) to address the changing market context in transportation. At the time of Mark Fields' departure, Ford's market capitalisation was $35.75 billion (Macrotrends.net, 2019a).

Meanwhile, Tesla, Inc., a California-based newcomer to the industry founded in 2003 and led by entrepreneur Elon Musk (established ~100 years after Ford), achieved a market capitalisation of $44 billion (Macrotrends.net, 2019b) in the same month that Mark Fields left Ford. One can imagine the conversations around the Ford boardroom table about the future of transportation and the valuation of Tesla at that time. How could an upstart insurgent like Tesla create so much value over such a short time whilst burning cash at a prodigious rate and producing only a small fraction of the vehicles made by Ford? What is Ford (and the rest of the incumbent industry) going to do to combat this insurgent? According to Musk (2017), Tesla was, at least in part, founded as a response to General Motors' termination of the EV1 electric car experiment in the early 2000s, having recalled the cars from consumers and then crushing them unceremoniously as is common with experimental programmes. In spite of Tesla's astronomic valuation ($44 billion at the time of writing against just over $40 billion for Ford), the company was not profitable and burning cash at an impressive rate. At the time of Fields' departure, it would have been entirely reasonable for Ford to assume that Tesla's position was untenable in the long run and that Ford could safely ignore the threat posed by Tesla. The typical argument used by the incumbent that the insurgent is insolvent and therefore doomed to fail ("but they're not making money!" is often used as a defence against mobilising for change). This same argument was used by many retailers as Amazon developed, not fully understanding that Amazon's lack of profitability was a function of reinvestment for growth, not poor management. Regardless of any scepticism about the sustainability of Tesla, Mark Fields was still fired from Ford. Ford's long-term survivability in its current form is a question mark (as is Tesla's).

Each company at that time was solving for something fundamentally different. Ford has (and still has) a long legacy to live up to and sold more than 6.6 million vehicles in 2017 as compared to Tesla's paltry 100,000 vehicles (Richter, 2018). A global company heavily invested in internal combustion engine (ICE) platforms with a vast global network of suppliers and a dealer-dependent business model, Ford is a big ship to turn. For investors, a bet on Ford is a bet on the historical model of the ICE-enabled transportation paradigm and a bet on Tesla is a much more uncertain bet on the future of transportation as whole, and, as we shall see, the role of battery technology in that future. As an incumbent, the pressure for Ford to extrapolate its core capabilities and extend its global position for ICE vehicles must be enormous, particularly as the uptake of electric vehicles is as uncertain as the current market size is small. Therefore, the short-term job of Ford can be seen as to maintain and grow its position in ICE globally whilst preparing for the future of transportation (but go faster on the latter) – this is the Y-axis focus. Tesla, on the other hand, is not burdened by this legacy and is playing a fundamentally different game.

Exhibit 20 represents a hypothetical "Trend Map" from Ford's perspective. On the Y-axis, the proximity to the core business is shown and on the X-axis is the degree of anticipated disruption to the core incumbent model. The lower left-hand quadrant represents the key trends that Ford needs to

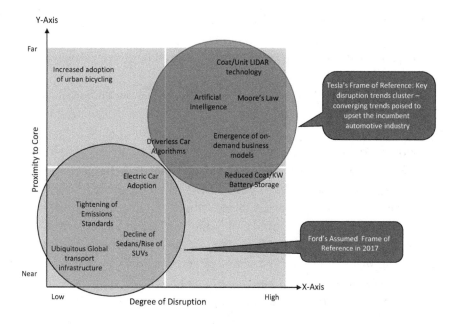

Exhibit 20 Trend map.

solve for in its core business and, moving to the upper right-hand quadrant, the key trends that are shaping the transportation industry as a whole in the long term. This model is a companion to the X/Y model shared in previous chapters and can be seen as an important outside-in overlay to that model. As you move across and up this map towards the upper right, naturally the uncertainty increases. It is reasonable to assume that the starting point for Ford under Mark Fields was the lower left-hand quadrant (i.e., get people excited about the future but invest in the present) and the upper right-hand quadrant is representative of Tesla's assumed focus, at least in part (i.e., get people excited about the future and deliver something new). This map is purely an illustration. It is worth noting that none of these trends act alone but rather in mutually reinforcing clusters. For example, the convergence of Moore's Law (i.e., the doubling of the number of transistors on a chip every ~2 years, thus doubling the processing power of a chip or roughly halving the cost per unit of processing power) with LIDAR (a technology used to create three-dimensional images using lasers) capability means that more sensors can be fitted to a vehicle with faster processing power at a lower cost. As these trends mature and the market adoption rate accelerates, the potential for disruption grows for the incumbents.

Ford's strategy to focus on emerging markets, SUVs and light trucks, fuel economy, connectivity, and put a toe into electric vehicles made sense in this context, and the market would have rewarded Ford, accordingly, were there not a Tesla.

The Tesla strategy, looking from the outside in, is more complex. As the insurgent, Tesla built its strategy and business model to deliberately undermine the core capabilities of the existing industry incumbents. At this point, it is important to ask: just what business is Tesla in? Is it a car company? A technology company? A battery storage company? A climate change company? All of the above? Tesla is made possible by the convergence of the many trends (and more besides) in the upper right-hand quadrant of Exhibit 20. When General Motors introduced EV1 in the 1990s as an experiment, it was too soon. A combination of mass-market adoption of consumer electronics driving the maturity of battery technology (currently based on lithium ion technology) at scale, Moore's Law, LIDAR, and machine learning all needed to click together at the right time and right cost to be competitive with the incumbent platform, ICE, notwithstanding the required changes in infrastructure to support EV technology at scale. Tesla was able to time its entry to the market to align very well to these trends, deliberately or not. In doing so, Tesla made several key decisions that set it apart from the incumbent model typified by Ford; consider Table 3.

As a car company, the Tesla business model is materially different from Ford, especially concerning its platform, distribution, and the supply chain. Tesla is an X-axis competitor to Ford's Y-axis focus. The point is that the model is materially different. Tesla understands the "Law of Diffusion of Innovation" very well (see Exhibit 21) and has based its core vehicle strategy on provision of a premium product, the Model S and the Model X, to a small but motivated market of innovators and early adopters at a premium price. As the market develops for electric vehicles, Tesla is moving along the bell curve and has introduced Model 3 (and soon the Model Y) to the early adopter and early majority segments of the market. While Tesla has had some difficulty getting its production under control, there is typically a large backorder for its vehicles. Tesla has played a significant role in stimulating the market for electric vehicles and enjoys, at the time of writing, leadership in the American market for electric cars and a leading share in sedans by value (Insideevs.com, 2019).

Tesla has also made, on the surface, some puzzling decisions. For example, the company has embraced "open source" and makes its patents available to other firms to copy (Schmidt, 2019). Why would a company encourage its

Table 3 Ford vs. Tesla Business Models

	Ford (incumbent)	Tesla (insurgent)
Distribution model	Dealership network	Direct via website
Dealerships	Independently owned, large footprint, hundreds of cars on the lot	Showcases, located in malls and small shopfronts – feature single car of each model
Market	Mass	Niche Premium (2017) later moving to niche mass (Model 3)
Range of products	Wide	Narrow
Target customer	Middle class – "late majority"	Affluent – "the innovator"
Supply chain	Global network of suppliers	"Full Stack" vertical integration (80%)
Manufacturing	Hybrid human and robotic	Mostly automated
Platform	ICE drivetrain/SUV focus	EV drivetrain/Sedan focus
Autonomous features	None	Self-driving capable
Transaction	Cash on delivery/financing	Deposit upfront/COD

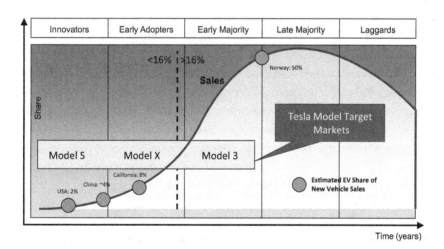

Exhibit 21 Diffusion of electric vehicles in selected markets.

competition to copy its innovations? The official reason for this is to stimulate the market for electric vehicles and displace as many ICE vehicles as possible as part of a broad vision to enable sustainable transport. As ICE incumbents and EV Insurgents pour billions of dollars into EV technology, the adoption of EVs and the displacement of ICE will accelerate to critical mass and move EV technology into the early majority, eventually crossing the 16% threshold typical for mass adoption , i.e., Maloney's Law (see Exhibit 21). Tesla is also far ahead of its competition and by making its technology widely available eventually makes the adoption of universal standards, on Tesla's terms, easier as EV, connectivity, and autonomous vehicles become mainstream and the battle for ownership of infrastructure gains momentum. Mass adoption looks more inevitable every day as the world's largest ICE automotive companies announce new products and platforms and companies such as Waymo, a division of Alphabet, the parent company of Google, Apple, and others make investments in EV/autonomous technology. Many countries have announced fleet objectives in favour of EV technology, including Norway with an aggressive goal of *all* new cars sold from 2025 will be "zero emissions" (Elbil.no, 2019). Tesla will certainly benefit from the first mover advantage having iterated through numerous generations of EV/autonomous technology before many companies introduce their first models into the market. However, as competition matures, the pressure on Tesla to make a profit and return value to shareholders will increase, particularly as incumbents begin to reach scale in production.

Is Tesla as a car company simply a transition strategy for the firm? If Tesla succeeds in driving other companies to mass adoption of EVs and autonomous vehicles, can they still win? One possible focus is to view Tesla as a battery/storage company and not a car company. Tesla's battery platform is supplied by a joint venture between Tesla and Panasonic at the famous "giga factories" in Nevada, New York State, and soon, China. As demand increases globally, the market for storage systems will increase exponentially. Tesla could bring battery production in-house and focus more on the supply of storage systems (note also that Tesla supplies storage systems for electricity utilities and residential photovoltaic systems). If Tesla's long-term strategy is based on storage and autonomous technology and not the car, some of the above decisions fit this strategy. Thus, once the world's automakers go "all in" on EV technology, Tesla is well-positioned to provide storage solutions and achieve its stated mission. It should also be noted that Tesla has invested heavily in infrastructure to support its growing consumer base in vehicles. In the long term, Tesla could become a key infrastructure player to support the inevitable growth of EV and autonomous vehicles. In short, Tesla appears to be solving for all of the above: 1) the disruption of ICE to enable a greener future, 2) stimulating demand to ensure mass adoption globally, and 3) preparing the groundwork to participate as a technology provider, storage company, and infrastructure player. Tesla is *driving* the trends to its desired future rather than simply *adjusting* to the emerging trends. As such, while Tesla as a car company looks quite fragile owing to its cash burn, the wider definition as described above would provide an opportunity for Tesla to participate as a key player in several key parts of the future transportation ecosystem it is striving to create.

Ford, on the other hand, is well behind the curve on these investments and faces many difficult decisions. In the months leading up to the time of writing, Ford has announced an exit from all but a few of its traditional sedan (car) lines (Sachgau and Naughton, 2019), excepting the iconic Mustang, in favour of light trucks and SUVs, a strong category for Ford. In the meantime, Ford is increasing its investment in a new portfolio of 40 EV and hybrid vehicles to be launched by 2022 (Carey and White, 2018) and is investing heavily in autonomous technology to catch up, including a significant investment with another latecomer, Volkswagen, in Argo, a Pittsburgh-based autonomous vehicle company, now valued at an almost astronomical $7 billion. (Hawkins, 2019).

To better understand the role of trends shaping the business, we find that using trend maps in combination with game theory (i.e., war gaming) to be the most effective method of insight harvesting from trend analysis. Any two-dimensional analysis of a complex market will be insufficient to fully understand how certain trends will converge and how these trends will influence the overall ecosystem. Without a trend map, a firm will very likely fall in the trap of putting too much emphasis on the lower left-hand quadrant trends, dismissing more disruptive trends as "irrelevant for now". This alone is unlikely to be sufficient precisely because it does not factor in how all of the stakeholders in the ecosystem will respond to various trends. This is the role of game theory and war gaming. War games are, unsurprisingly, derived from military applications (i.e., what will the enemy do if we attack *here*?). As a business tool, war games can be highly complex and quantitative or simple and qualitative.

The essence of war gaming is to discover how the market will respond simultaneously to key "outer edge" trends as they unfold and converge with other trends as well as how all key stakeholders (incumbents and insurgents, customers, suppliers, policy makers, etc.) will react over time to externalities/ trends on one hand and all of the decisions of the above stakeholders on the other. War games are essentially a simulation of a market, over time, factoring in a combination of trends (derived from the trend map) with a live (or AI-simulated) role play of how each actor in the ecosystem will behave. This method is cumulative with all of the information at one point in time carried forward into the future as the clock moves forward in predetermined increments, i.e., "rounds". War games help derive deep insights into how decisions propagate through the market, how best to time investments and inform strategies, and at what point will disruption become a clear and present threat to the existing business model. Imagine if Kodak had applied game theory in 1974 to model how digital imaging would evolve over the next 30 years? Had their game been constrained only to "known" players such as Agfa and Fuji, the results would have only been moderately interesting. However, had Kodak included an extrapolation of trends such as Moore's Law (for imaging purposes how many pixels could be fit on the imaging chip?) and a variety of other stakeholders such as telecommunications players, consumer electronics players, computer companies, consumers, content providers, etc., they would have been able to predict with some accuracy the point in the future when digital imaging would replace film at scale and, importantly, the likely applications for digital imaging. Armed with this information, Kodak could have made different choices to maintain relevance, assuming the company had the political will to change.

Game theory, when coupled with analysis of marginal economics, can be particularly useful. For example, we worked with an electricity distributor to help them understand the potential impact of disruption created by the uptake of rooftop solar cells (PVs) coupled with battery storage systems. The guiding question was "at what point will PVs upset the economics of the existing business model and how will the market respond to the change?" The client assumed a "slow burn" 25-year disruption based on an inside-out estimation of the decision cycles on assets such as substations (asset life for equipment can be 30–50 years). We took a contrarian view and suggested that the company had no more than 5 years to make the adjustment based on the argument that even linear extrapolation of the current adoption of PV and storage technology would upset their economics within 5 years, i.e., the most conservative possible case. We agreed that at some point as the peak demand for electricity rises owing to climate change (this factor drives infrastructure build) and average demand falls (owing to more efficient appliances and price increases) that the model would eventually unravel, driving marginal cost to unsustainable levels (i.e., where price increases could no longer keep pace with cost increases). To test our collective thinking, very much oversimplified here, we built an economic model and a war game to determine the adoption rate of the PV technology and how the industry would evolve over time (including the incumbent value chain, regulators, consumers, and the insurgent ecosystem – PV and storage companies (e.g., Tesla), technology companies (e.g., Google), and many others). We simulated 30 years of change in the market in the game, at each stage (time period) estimating the impact on the economic model of the company. Over 100 people were involved in the exercise, run over 2 days. What we discovered was profoundly interesting. When combining all of the available trends, we learned that each trend accelerated all of the others in a sort of hyper-loop. We also learned that the take up of PV technology would have a dramatic impact on the business in *less* than 5 years and that the company was not well-positioned for the change having committed to a 10-year asset plan. As more consumers went partially or totally off-grid, the marginal cost would increase driving up prices and leading to more consumers going off-grid in a vicious cycle (for the incumbent) or virtuous cycle (for the insurgent). These insights led to a complete rethink of the company's business model and helped inform regulators how to make a more orderly market transition for exposed consumers as the adoption rate of PVs accelerated.

Overall, the lesson for strategists on both sides of the incumbent and insurgent coin is simple. If you are among the 90% of companies that believe your environmental context to be increasingly unstable, you have to think differently and use different methods to surface actionable insights.

References

Carey, N & White, J, 2018, Ford plans $11 billion investment, 40 electrified vehicles by 2022, *Reuters*, viewed 20 August 2019, https://www.reuters.com/article/us-autoshow-detroit-ford-motor/ford-plans-11-billion-investment-40-electrified-vehicles-by-2022-idUSKBN1F30YZ.

Ebil.no, Norwegian EV policy: Norway is leading the way for a transition to zero emission in transport, *Norsk elbilforening*, viewed 20 August 2019, https://elbil.no/english/norwegian-ev-policy/.

Felton, R, 2017, Why Mark Fields was fired, *Jalopnik*, viewed 20 August 2019, https://jalopnik.com/why-mark-fields-was-fired-1795431562.

Hawkins, A, 2019, Ford-VW alliance expands to include autonomous and electric vehicles, *The Verge*, viewed 20 August 2019, https://www.theverge.com/2019/7/12/20690722/ford-vw-alliance-self-driving-argo-investment-valuation.

Loveday, S, 2019, Inside Evs, *Wade Malone*, viewed 20 August 2019, https://insideevs.com/news/362819/ev-sales-scorecard-july-2019.

Macrotrends.net, 2019a, Ford motor market cap 2006–2019, *Macrotrends LLC*, viewed 20 August 2019, https://www.macrotrends.net/stocks/charts/F/ford-motor/market-cap.

Macrotrends.net, 2019b, Tesla market cap 2009–2019 | TSLA, *Macrotrends LLC*, viewed 20 August 2019, https://www.macrotrends.net/stocks/charts/TSLA/tesla/market-cap.

Musk, E, 2017, viewed 19 August 2019, https://twitter.com/elonmusk/status/873116351316938753.

Richter, F, 2018, Tesla delivers 100, 000 cars in 2017 but misses model 3 goals, *Statista, Inc.*, viewed 20 August 2019, https://www.statista.com/chart/12415/tesla-deliveries-and-model-3-production/.

Sachgau, O & Naughton, K, 2019, Ford will close six European plants as part of global downsizing, *Bloomberg L.P.*, viewed 26 November 2019, https://www.bloomberg.com/news/articles/2019-06-27/ford-to-eliminate-20-of-european-workforce-in-sweeping-overhaul.

Schmidt, B, 2019, Tesla's free-to-use patents are all about sustainability – and strength, viewed 20 August 2019, https://thedriven.io/2019/02/04/tesla-patents-free-to-use-sustainable-strength/.

10 | Implications for strategy design

In writing this book, one of my goals was to create a blueprint for strategy development to help incumbents pick up some of the characteristics of insurgents, in particular how they think about the world and build strategy. Using the Insurgence X/Y framework, our model for strategy design and innovation, we seek to help business leaders on both sides of the coin (incumbents and insurgents alike) to improve their thinking and identify new ways to compete and, hopefully, to view disruption as an opportunity more than a threat. Fundamentally, however, it is the incumbent we wish to influence to behave and operate more like insurgents.

In his seminal book, "The Lean Start-Up" (Reis, 2011), Eric Reis made the case that start-ups need to have in place lean disciplines, not just to develop products but also to get as close to customers as possible in a shared learning process that allows them to experiment and iterate over rapid cycles to allow the business to rapidly achieve scale amidst a high degree of uncertainty. "The Lean Start Up" approach is now mainstream and in use in large enterprises as well as start-ups, being applied to product development and other disciplines where rapid learning cycles can be applied. Published in 2011, Reis' approach codified the importance of "velocity to scale" for start-ups and is an excellent guidebook and methodology for the would-be insurgent.

Almost concurrently, Roger Martin and A. G. Lafley wrote a book called "Playing to Win" (Martin and Lafley, 2013), making the case that strategy is essentially a set of choices that can be outlined in a series of five simple, but powerful, questions for leaders to contemplate in making strategy, namely:

1. What is our winning aspiration?
2. Where will we play?

3. How will we win where we have chosen to play?
4. What capabilities must be in place to win?
5. What management systems are required to ensure the capabilities are in place?

Having answered these questions, and applying granular analysis to support the choices, the strategy becomes clear and how best to deploy resources to execute on these choices defines the plan. Published in 2013, this book has become almost a definitive resource for strategists and, like The Lean Start Up, an excellent guidebook and methodology for incumbents in *stable contexts*.

Insurgence is intended to bridge the gap between the above concepts to help incumbents better focus their resources on "the velocity of disruption" brought about by unstable conditions and context. The X/Y framework encapsulates the major elements described in the preceding chapters in this section of the book, a summary of which is described below, described first from the point of view of the inside-out incumbent:

1. Y-Axis – The relentless pursuit of "more" (key focus of "strategy") – strong Y-axis bias
2. X-Axis – The inflexibility of the incumbent's business model ("a constant")
3. In the Box – Extrapolation of "core capabilities" and optimisation of the existing business model
4. Customer Frontier – "thou shalt not self-cannibalise"
5. Key Trends – Focus on the "known"

Described from the point of view of the outside-in insurgent, the emphasis is very different:

1. Y-Axis – Pursuit of the minimum viable product (iterate and refine)
2. X-Axis – Build a scalable and differentiated business model (iterate as needed) – strong X-axis bias
3. In the Box – Build capabilities that are distinct from the incumbent competition (iterate as needed)
4. Customer Frontier – Focus on customer proximity
5. Key Trends – Focus on the convergence of key trends on the horizon

In other words, the core elements are the same, but the emphasis is different and yields very different results. We find that successful insurgents tend to drive disruption via 1) an X-axis orientation (i.e., the business model and its underlying assumptions are different), 2) customer proximity (i.e., a focus on innovation at the customer frontier), 3) *convergence* of trends on the horizon, and 4) the development of distinctly different capabilities (as compared to the incumbent). Can an incumbent, having already achieved scale, choose to operate as an insurgent? We think the answer is yes. We believe that disruption is also a choice, one often made out of wilful ignorance, lazy thinking, and the inability to "let-go" of baseline assumptions on the part of the incumbent, i.e., controlled flight into terrain. None of these things are fundamentally outside the control of the incumbent firm. That's great news. Things in the control of a firm can be changed.

To illustrate the application of the Insurgence framework, we will use the case of Lego to show how an incumbent can think fundamentally differently about the business and drive transformation in a turbulent environment.

I first "discovered" Lego as a company quite by accident. To be clear, I was always aware of Lego but never gave it much thought until my son's tenth birthday. Before I get to that, from the time he was about 5 years old, Lego was always a staple gift at every birthday party, with an average of two Lego sets out of ten gifts. When he was young, we used to limit the number of kids invited to the birthday party to ten in total. His ninth birthday was no exception. He received two Lego sets (I can't recall which ones, probably Lego City). After helping him assemble these sets, I didn't pay Lego any particular attention. I should mention that in my neighbourhood at that time, there was a sort of gift-giving psychology at work in selecting Lego sets for birthday parties. Roughly speaking, traditional Lego sets fall into three price brackets: 1) under $30, 2) $30–60, and 3) above $60. If you bring one of the small under $30 sets to a birthday party, you fall into the "cheapo" category; after all, an $18 set doesn't get you much, maybe a mini-figure on a motorcycle. Above $60 and you fall in the "pretentious" category and make everyone else feel like a cheapo when the gifts are opened. As such, like with Goldilocks and the Three Bears, the middle category is the safest. Apologies for the digression but that adds up to say $100 total spend on Lego for his ninth birthday.

The next year, my son's tenth birthday, was different. First, clever boy that he is, it was decided that he would have a *joint* birthday party with a friend in a clever ploy to circumvent our rule, bringing the maximum number of kids from 10 to 20. Since the other boy's birthday was the same weekend, how could we say no? This was in 2014 when the first Lego movie came out. It was a forgone conclusion that the joint birthday party, in early March of that year, would include the boys taking their friends to the Lego movie and, obviously, that the party would have a Lego theme. That's what we did. Now what does EVERY guest (20) bring to a Lego birthday party? You guessed it, Lego. That's 20 Lego sets. A great test of my theory of birthday gift psychology, almost all of the sets were in the $30–60 category. The birthday was a big success and after what seemed like a 12-hour shift of putting Lego together with my son the next day (my hands never recovered), we had what seemed like a whole room full of new (some duplicates) sets assembled and arranged on a shelf – most of them remain there today, the remainder are in plastic boxes, an exercise in entropy.

The next morning sitting in my office, reflecting on the weekend, I started to think about Lego as a company, something I hadn't considered previously. First, I was amazed by the total "share of birthday" that Lego represented that year, 100%. Second, the "total spend" was also suitably impressive; third, and perhaps most important, it was declared the "best birthday ever" by the boys. The numbers were equally interesting and described in Table 4.

As I sat in my office, doodling these numbers on a notepad, I was amazed to see that, in just one year, Lego was able to garner a 15x increase in total sales from a single (albeit combined) birthday party! How was this possible? This grabbed my attention and I started to research Lego in more detail.

Lego was established in Denmark in the 1940s and is famous for, amongst other things, its interlocking brick system, mini-figures, and themed playsets, including the popular Star Wars and Marvel sets depicting scenes from the films. Given the power of the brand and the ubiquity of its products, it is difficult to imagine the reader not having had some exposure to Lego from a product viewpoint. What I discovered through my research was that Lego, circa 2003, was in significant trouble and very close to bankruptcy, having generated a loss of approximately of US$240 million on US$1,020 billion of revenue (*The Economist*, 2006). Lego, at the time a classic incumbent, typified the "more" ethos described above that many incumbents fall prey to. Building on a strong iconic brand, but operating in a relatively stagnant market for toys at the time, the business overextended itself into numerous

Table 4 Year-On-Year Comparison of Total Spend on Lego

Year/item	Ninth birthday	Tenth birthday
# Lego sets × avg. price = X	2 sets @ $50 = $100	20 sets @ $50 = $1000
# Movie tickets × avg. price = X	$0	20 tickets @ $25 = $500
Total	$100 total spend	$1500 total spend

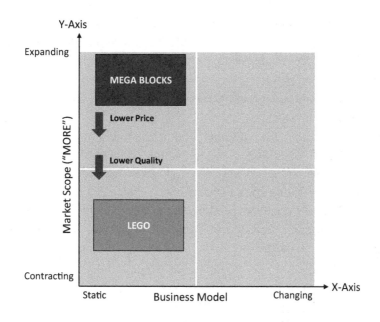

Exhibit 22 Lego circa 2003.

adjacent businesses, including theme parks, significantly proliferated the number of stock keeping units (SKUs) to the point that its distribution channels were choking on unsold inventory and was opening Lego brand stores without adequately understanding the channel dynamics (i.e., channel conflict) created by competing with retail partners (e.g., Target and Walmart) (Ashcroft, 2014). Concurrently, having recently lost patent protection on its interlocking brick system, Lego was, for the first time, under some pressure from traditional competition in the "construction toy" category. These competitors, including Mega Bloks, a copycat competitor offering inferior quality products at a lower price at the time, were putting pressure on Lego's traditional customer base and peeling away price-sensitive and quality-indifferent customers. Mega Bloks was a moderate threat, and in spite of Lego's efforts to defend its system in the courts (largely unsuccessful), Mega Bloks was able to take share and grow to the #2 position in the category at the time. See Exhibit 22, positioning the Lego circa 2003 situation on the Insurgence X/Y model. Note the following:

1. Lego sought to extrapolate existing capabilities to achieve "more" on the Y-axis leading to a proliferation of products and adjacent businesses

2. Core capabilities included: 1) Lego brand, 2) brick system and close tolerance manufacturing, 3) global distribution, including channel partners, and 4) consumer marketing
3. Incumbent competition (Mega Bloks) attacking Lego on the Y-axis offering a me-too product and challenging Lego on price but with a noticeably inferior product
4. Limited focus on the customer frontier, instead prioritising extracting more value from existing customers with a strong product focus
5. Business defined as "Construction Toy Company" focused primarily on boys ages 6–11 (though not exclusively)
6. Business model relatively fixed in core business (make, sell, and distribute Lego products via third-party distribution channels and a small number of direct channels)

The turnaround of Lego, led by former management consultant, Jorgen Vig Knudstorp, involved a radical rethink of the company's strategy and model. Mr. Knudstorp and his team had to radically refocus the business to reduce complexity, remove costs, and refocus the business on customers. The basic recipe of the short-term turnaround included the following key elements:

1. Complexity reduction: elimination of unprofitable SKUs and lines of business, e.g., selling off theme parks to private equity
2. Refocus of the business on the "Brick", the essential core capability of Lego
3. Slow down retail expansion (Lego branded stores)
4. Remove redundant costs by shrinking the workforce
5. Rediscover the customer (channel) and the end consumer

Exhibit 23 shows these decisions plotted on each axis.

All of these decisions are typical of the turnaround of an incumbent. In the Lego case, there was no significant insurgent disruptor on the scene at that time undermining the business other than Mega Bloks, an inferior Y-axis competitor. As such, the majority of the problems were of Lego's own making, aside from the soft market conditions for the toy category at that time. My interpretation of what happened next is what follows. I should note that this is framed somewhat differently than the "official story".

As noted above, one of the most powerful questions a business can ask is "what are we solving for?" Prior to Mr. Knudstorp coming on the scene,

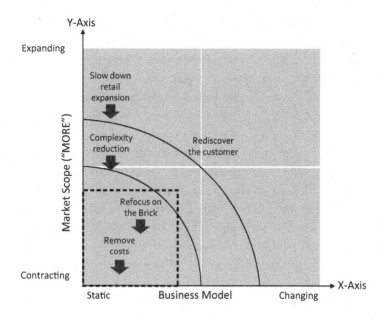

Exhibit 23 LEGO turnaround priorities.

the business seems to have been defined largely as a "construction toy company" aimed at boys between the ages of 6 and 11 years old. What a toy company does is makes and sells toys, of course. What a business does – particularly an incumbent that has a high opinion of itself, a strong brand following, and a loyal legacy customer base in an attempt to sell MORE toys. The "toy company" definition is very constraining and is a good representation of what a Y-axis competitor does. Anyone who has experienced Lego knows that the value Lego brings to consumers is not about the "toy". Once the Lego set is built and the "toy" is complete, it becomes a lot less fun to play with and often ends up on the shelf. In the first Lego movie, one of the subplots focused on the father building a Lego city in his basement. In the film, the father would not let his boy play with the city or pull apart the bricks. It went so far as to suggest that the Lego bricks were all connected with super glue (i.e., the "Kragle") to prevent his son from taking it apart. The apparent lesson from the film being, "where's the fun in that?" The beginning of the process (the building of the original set) and the end of the process (the assembly of unique creations from pieces borrowed from old sets drawn from the plastic bin) are more fun. Anyone who has actually played with Lego understands that it is all about "creating, designing, and building" and not the "toy" itself.

113

The brick is a platform for the building experience, not so much a toy. I believe that Lego, pre-2003, behaved like an incumbent toy company.

The key question, in my mind, is what does a "create, design, and build" company look like, building off of a platform (the brick), and what is the business model of such a company? This (re)discovery at Lego was achieved by visiting consumers at the customer frontier and conducting focus groups to understand the contexts in which the products were used; this is known as ethnographic research. It turns out that the product has incredible resonance beyond boys between the ages of 6 and 11. Artists, architects, teachers, engineers, adults, consultants, girls (yes!), etc., all have different use cases for the platform, such as manufacturing simulation, a medium for art, a teaching aid, a team-building tool, etc. Through this process, Lego discovered that the platform itself need not be physical (i.e., plastic) but can also be digital. For example, Lego Digital Designer (no longer supported) was a tool that allowed amateur designers to choose from any of the bricks in the entire Lego library using a PC application to build a virtual model and, once complete, to have the model shipped as a "custom set". The business model need not be the same as every other toy company (make, market, sell, etc.) but can be expanded in different ways to meet the needs of customers beyond the transaction at the point of sale (still relevant, but a starting point, not an end point). By opening up the definition of Lego, the company frees itself to redefine its relationship with customers at the frontier, develop alternative business models on the X-axis, and create new products on the Y-axis. Each of these changes requires new distinctive capabilities; these are illustrated in Exhibit 24.

Lego has become highly customer-proximate, opening up product development and innovation, marketing and creative processes to consumers across numerous related platforms all based on the brick (both physical and digital). These platforms include games, films, robotics, coding, architecture, consulting, theme parks, etc. Through co-creation with Lego consumers and fans, Lego gains a tremendous amount of insight into what people are interested in, how the platform is being used, and gains significant data that can be translated into products. For example, Lego Ideas offers a platform for Lego fans (Lego Ideas is aimed primarily at adult fans) and claims to have over 1,000,000 fans crowdsourcing ideas from all over the world (Lego.com, 2018). The ideas generated by this community of customers has generated dozens of new products over the past decade. The fans are part of the design process which helps Lego generate invaluable insights into what and how

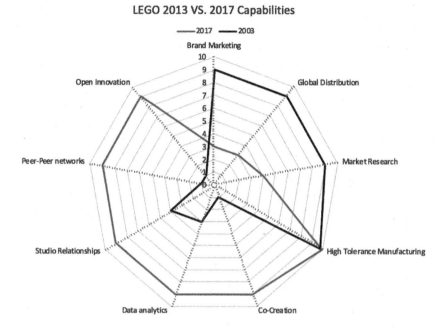

Exhibit 24 LEGO capability map.

consumers are designing, building, and creating using the Lego platform. The data generated is marketing and product development gold.

The traditional "fortress" surrounding Lego is non-existent. The boundaries of Lego extend far out into the world of their customers, partners, fans, friends, etc. Another example, the Lego Mindstorms robotics platform is built around an open software concept that encourages coders (even hackers) to challenge, improve, and modify the code to make the Mindstorm experience more valuable to the community. While initially reluctant to open up the platform, Lego did take the risk, making the bet that it was better to have the hackers in the tent than outside it. The programme has been a big success (Iglesias, 2018). Innovation, drawn from customer proximity at the customer frontier, leads to entirely new product and service opportunities, not just Y-axis line extensions. By contrast, according to Forbes, 80% of all product and service innovations in business are line extensions.

On the supply side, Lego as a company is also a platform. The company's openness extends to numerous strategic partnerships including franchise partnerships (e.g., Disney, Marvel, etc.) that provide a clever alternative distribution model for franchise brands and a great way for Lego to stay current with what people are interested in. Also included are the movies and TV shows (e.g., Lego Masters). Most of these partnerships are symbiotic. It is hard to imagine the Star Wars brand without Lego. The principles of openness, interactivity, and creation are embedded in a web of mutually reinforcing engagement channels, anchored by strategic relationships (Exhibit 25).

Like McDonald's Australia, described in Chapter 7, Lego is highly experimental and willing to take projects to scale, learn, and rapidly sunset them (and try again), if not successful. One example, Lego Universe, introduced in 2010 and rapidly scaled to millions of customers, then shut down in 2012 after disappointing results, a brave call. The company now routinely and unceremoniously sunsets experiments that don't land successfully in the market. The company now boasts more than a dozen video games, many tied into franchises (e.g., Star Wars, Batman, etc.). These include Lego Worlds, a reboot of the Universe concept introduced in 2015.

Lego has reaped tremendous rewards from its transformation. In 2014, Lego became the world's largest "toy" company, edging out Mattel for the #1 position, and is currently the most valuable toy brand worth more than $7 billion at the time of writing (Handley, 2018). As the company evolves, there is a strong focus on melding together its physical and digital experiences (Milne, 2019). However, in recent years, the toy market is again unstable amidst a continuously changing retail landscape, notably the collapse of Toys R Us in

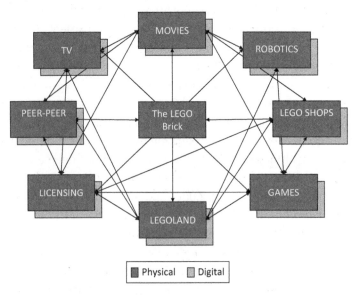

Exhibit 25 Mutually reinforcing platforms.

2018 and the emergence of online retailers like Amazon. Lego, despite difficult years in 2016–2018 to adjust to these factors, has returned to revenue and profit growth and is growing market share (Lego, 2019).

Lego is what we call a hybrid company, a company that was able to transcend its roots as a classic Y-axis incumbent and behave much more like an X-axis insurgent. Lego typifies the main characteristics of an insurgent bringing together a willingness to "solve for something different", embrace customer proximity, unfreeze the X-axis with material alterations to the business model, and create new and distinctive capabilities, many of these fully transparent to outside contributors, including customers.

Unfortunately, most incumbents are unable to make these sweeping changes. One benefit that Lego had was its near extinction event in 2003, i.e., the "burning platform" that refocused its efforts. Nothing creates focus like a crisis and it can be hard to drive change without an existential threat. As mentioned above, most strategy processes are budget-driven and are built on the fundamental assumption that the business will grow come what may. While it is the job of leaders to find new sources of growth, new growth cannot come from an indefinite flogging of existing products, line extensions, and a fixed business model. For firms without an obvious external threat, change becomes difficult. Many incumbent firms slip slowly, year after year, each year introducing the next big strategy that will restore the company to growth. Yet these firms almost always make the same mistakes, assuming that cost-cutting (in the box) and product extensions (Y-axis focus) will turn the tide.

We work with many not-for-profit (NFP), mission-focused, or traditional member-based organisations across the economy including health care, financial services, real estate, technology, etc. We find that many of these organisations are especially vulnerable to incumbent strategy design mindsets. Designed in the predigital age, the business models for many NFP organisations are becoming obsolete as their context becomes less stable owing to a variety of factors as customer behaviour evolves and insurgent competition intensifies. As each successive generation of leadership comes on stream, these organisations tend to focus on: 1) continuation of the mission and 2) perpetuation of the existing business model. The assumption of perpetuity seems to be a key leadership driver in most firms, particularly NFPs. As a result, year after year the NFP model loses money, each year shrinking a little bit more amidst attempts to introduce new products. NFP organisations are almost always Y-axis incumbents and seldom, if ever, fundamentally rethink their business models and capabilities. Sometimes this can go on for years. Having "banked" surpluses from good years, these organisations often have significant cash and property assets underwriting a dying business model. Usually a financial projection can be created that shows management and the board almost the exact month and year that the model will collapse, forcing closure or combination with another organisation.

How does this happen? It's very simple. Their strategy processes do not typically include a rethink of the business model. In many cases, the assumptions underpinning these business models (e.g., Aged Care: people will retire at 55 years old, Auto Club: cars break down, Industry Association: membership brings prestige, etc.) may be decades old (or even longer). Add to this a constitution that ensures a "forever" focus on a single and unchanging mission, you have a recipe for eventual disruption. The strategy process in these organisations does not allow for these kinds of questions, instead operating on the assumption that current core capabilities can be forever extrapolated to find new opportunities. Insurgence applies to NFP organisations as much as for-profit firms, perhaps more. Similarly, government organisations, under pressure to deliver ever more with less resources, eventually find themselves at a breaking point where service quality collapses and private sector alternatives become more attractive, without a significant rethink of the model.

Any firm with an incumbent-based, budget-driven, Y-axis strategy process in the 21st century needs to rethink its approach as a matter of urgency. As the core assumptions underpinning your business model fall into obsolescence in light of an unstable context, your business becomes more and more fragile and subject to disruption. Doing "more" with "less" will seldom be sufficient to address the problem. It's hard work to rethink the foundations of your business. In summary:

1. **What are you solving for?** – Lego reframed their business by redefining their focus on the "create" experience instead of "selling toys". This shift had a profound impact on their ability to open up to new markets (Y-axis) and build alternative business models (X-axis). For mission-based organisations – is your mission still relevant?
2. **Outside-in focus** – Your strategy process cannot be budget-driven and must instead triangulate competition (incumbent and insurgent), evolution of customer needs and behaviours, and the combination of "edge of horizon" trends.

3. **Assumptions are key** – All firms are based on a series of assumptions. Your baseline assumptions about your business and the market in which you operate are one of the most important variables you can work with. Most businesses are unaware of their baseline assumptions much less understand when these assumptions hold true and under what conditions those assumptions lose validity. By discovering and testing these assumptions you can better understand your vulnerability to disruption. If you don't, insurgents will discover and exploit your baseline assumptions at your expense.

4. **Most disruption comes from the X-axis, not the Y-axis** – While product disruption is always a possibility, it is more likely that business model disruption will (X-axis) drive disruption (sometimes both, e.g., Tesla, Apple). Strategy processes that "freeze" the business model and do not consider changes on the X-axis are insufficient

5. **Core capability is not enough** – The incumbent mindset of forever extrapolating existing capabilities to find Y-axis growth opportunities will eventually fail. In the Lego case, we saw how the company refocused its capability set to pivot the business into the future. New and distinctive capabilities need to be developed, bought, or co-opted to move the business on the X-axis.

6. **Operate at the customer frontier** – Don't be paralysed by the fear of self-cannibalisation. Your strategy process must be deeply informed by (ideally with) your customers out at the edge of your offering. Find the customers retreating away at the fastest rate, understand them, co-create with them. Mass-market consumer research is usually not sufficient to draw out emerging insights to help you find new territory.

References

Ashcroft, J, 2014, The Lego case study 2014, *John Ashcroft and Company*, viewed 21 August 2019, https://hacerlobien.net/lego/Grupol-012-Case-Study.pdf.

Handley, L, 2018, How marketing built Lego into the world's favourite toy brand, *CNBC LLC*, viewed 21 August 2019, https://cnbc.com/2018/04/27/lego-marketing-strategy-made-it-world-favorite-toy-brand.html.

Iglesias, O, 2018, Why your company should embrace co-creation, *Esade Business and Law School, Forbes*, viewed 21 August 2019, https://forbes.com/sites/esade/2018/09/24/why-your-company-should-embrace-co-creation/#82b31da1bddf.

Lego.com, 2018, Celebrating 10 years of crowdsourcing and co-creation with Lego fans, *Lego System A/S*, viewed 21 August 2019, https://lego.com/en-sg/aboutus/news-room/2018/november/ideas-10th-anniversary.

Martin, R & Lafley, A, 2013, *Playing to Win*. Harvard Business Review Press, Boston, Massachusetts.

Milne, R, 2019, FT.com, Lego defies toy industry woes to return to growth, *Financial Times*, viewed 21 August 2019, https://ft.com/content/101d7dda-3a69-11e9-b72 b-2c7f526ca5d0.

Ries, E, 2011, *The Lean Startup: How Today's Entrepreneurs Use Continuous Innovation to Create Radically Successful Businesses*. Crown Publishing Group. New York: Crown Business, [2011] ©2011.

The Economist, 2006, Lego's turnaround: picking up the pieces, the venerable toymaker has recovered after a mistaken over-diversification, *The Economist*, viewed 21 August 2019, https://economist.com/business/2006/10/26/picking-up-the-pieces.

Implications for innovation

Few topics in business are less well understood than innovation. In our experience, even asking the question "what is innovation?" amongst any group of people, particularly innovation specialists, will yield almost as many answers as people in the room. Yet, one thing we can all agree on is the importance of innovation and its relative degree of difficulty (i.e., high and hard). Innovation theory seems to go from one fad to the next over each decade, often seeking to find answers from great innovators and generalising their insights to be applied universally. I find it challenging to keep up with all of this but at the same time feel that innovation has never been more important for firms seeking to find ways to compete and stay relevant and ahead of the curve in an increasingly fast-moving and uncertain future.

Having spoken to dozens of innovation "experts" and practitioners around the globe over the last decade or so, there is some consensus, however, regarding what innovation is *for*, if not what it *is*. Most practitioners agree that innovation exists to "apply know-how to solve problems that create value, however defined". "Value, however defined", is important because, as we have discovered, each firm is *solving for* something different. At the highest level, value for a listed firm may be biased towards shareholders (though exclusive focus on shareholders is coming out of fashion), whereas for a mission-focused firm, value might be defined in terms of achieving, for example, health outcomes. It is worth noting that, for our purposes, "solving a problem" can be used interchangeably with "finding an opportunity" but hereafter we will use the term "problem" to describe both states. The problem to be solved may vary significantly depending on the context a firm finds itself in and therefore the methods used to solve the problem may vary significantly as well. Sometimes, problems are unclear and vague, and, at other times, problems are well understood and crystal clear. The "application of know-how" implies that innovation builds on a body of existing knowledge, though often applied in an entirely different context. Innovation definitions often place emphasis on "new" or "novel" approaches to solve problems. This strikes me as sometimes, but not always, true as some innovations result from very small changes to existing know-how, others apply existing know-how to new context, and still others may be completely novel. Other definitions sometimes focus attention on "invention". Inventions are always new and for the most part innovative, though an invention that fails to solve a problem that creates meaningful value would not fall into our definition of innovation.

Many organisations fail at innovation because they are unable to define both the problem to be solved and the value to be created. Additionally, some firms are sometimes unable to define who will benefit from the innovation other than the firm itself. A lack of clarity on these dimensions amounts to a fishing expedition in an uncharted sea without a hook and with no idea if there are even fish in the water. Surely the fisherman could better spend his or her time on something else? Exhibit 26 describes this problem below.

This is precisely the focus of many incumbent innovation programmes. The organisation agrees that innovation is important, even essential, deploys resource, usually under a head of innovation, that then seeks to add value by innovating everything, achieving nothing. Often solving the wrong problem. One client we worked with, a global manufacturing business famous for its innovation capability, reached out to us for help because the business' growth had stalled amidst increasing competition and maturity of its product lines. The share price was stagnant and, whilst revenue was down, profitability was stable and growing marginally faster than revenue. This business was losing market share in five out of seven of its divisions. Having a reputation for innovation, we asked the client to show us the business' innovation activity to better understand how resources were being deployed to solve the growth problem.

Initially, we were impressed. Every employee was encouraged to set aside time for innovation, amounting to up to 1 day per week for some roles and at least 2–3 hours per day for others. A sophisticated internal crowdsourcing platform was in place to gather employee innovation ideas and a sort of market was in place for employees to vote for the best ideas by spending "virtual money" on the best ideas. It was cool. There was an innovation team consisting of a senior manager, several analysts (mainly supporting the software), and several six-sigma black belts working on projects across the business.

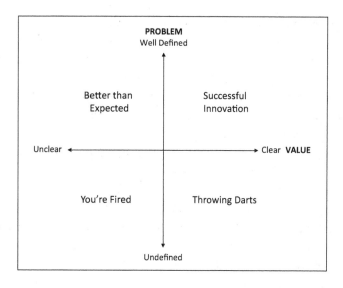

Exhibit 26 Value/problem matrix.

Overall, this was a very professional and well-organised team. However, when we looked at the programme, we noticed several things immediately. First, the number of ideas that flowed from their crowdsourcing efforts through to implementation was very low (note: employees were encouraged to search for opportunities in the business and make suggestions for improvement); less than 1% of opportunities evaluated made it through to implementation planning, and fewer still were allocated budget and resources (i.e., in flight) and organised as projects. That said the flow of ideas was impressive with hundreds coming each month but the innovation team was unable to cope with the backlog of ideas and senior leadership lacked the time and inclination to review and fund the best ideas owing to lack of confidence in results amidst a challenging business environment.

The six-sigma team was more successful, working on process improvement opportunities across the business with an impressive track record of efficiency improvements and cost savings, easily generating 3–4x ROI on the investment in these resources. Unfortunately, the business suffered from a lack of clarity regarding what problem it was trying to solve with its innovation efforts and how best to define value. Any reader can immediately see the problem. The business is not growing, and market share is sliding! As far as we could tell much of the innovation effort was unfocused and entirely bottom-up (the crowdsourcing) and the part that was successful (the six-sigma team) was focused on efficiency and cost, not growth. In other words, almost all of the discretionary resource deployed to innovation was pointed in the wrong direction. The same applied to product development (not included in the innovation team). For example, product development innovation hubs were located in mature markets and overindexed to product line extensions on mature products and not on genuinely new products. Overall, the business was not deploying discretionary resources to drive growth (the problem and the definition of value creation). This is a common problem with innovation. A big part of the solution was to refocus and redeploy these resources to find new growth opportunities.

Consider Exhibit 27. On one axis we show a spectrum of top-down vs. bottom-up. Top-down being specific problems defined by senior management to be solved, bottom-up being many problems solved by many people very organically, as seen in the above example. On the other axis, we show inside-out vs. outside-in. Inside-out refers to innovation driven purely by company objectives and outside-in refers to innovation driven by externalities.

In the upper right-hand quadrant (top-down/outside-in), there are two famous examples that come to mind: 1) the Apollo Program and 2) the Manhattan Project. Each of these innovation programmes were designed to solve a very specific problem related to a competitive threat (i.e., outside-in). The programmes were top-down in nature and defined and funded at

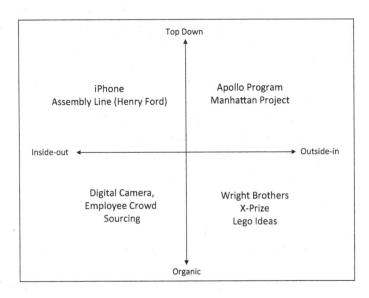

Exhibit 27 Top-down vs. bottom-down innovation.

the national government level. A clear objective (e.g., "beat the Nazis to the bomb") was defined. These programmes were successful because the problem was clear and adequate, and almost unlimited, and resources were deployed to solve these problems. These were "big bets".

In the upper left-hand quadrant (top-down/inside-out), there are again two famous examples: 1) Henry Ford's development of the assembly line and 2) the iPhone and the app store. These innovation programmes were developed not to meet an external threat but to solve a particular problem for the consumer (e.g., availability of affordable cars to the masses). Again, these programmes were clearly defined, well-funded, and incredibly successful but also "big bets".

In the lower left-hand quadrant (bottom-up/inside-out) we have the example described above, the employee crowdsourcing of ideas. In the example, we saw that the programme was unsuccessful because the problem was not well defined and resources were diffuse across hundreds of people, choking into a bottleneck where a few people were expected to sift through hundreds of ideas. Had the problem (growth) been clearly defined, perhaps the outcome would have been marginally better.

In the lower right-hand quadrant, (bottom-up/outside-in), examples that come to mind are 1) X-prize (xprize.org) and 2) controlled flight. In the case of controlled flight, the problem was widely known, and the technology was mature to the extent that the innovation was inevitable. The race between Louis Bleriot of France and Wilbur and Orville Wright of the United States (amongst dozens of others) created a competition to be the first to solve the problem of safe powered and controlled flight. Again, this problem was clearly defined but the solution implementation was very much organic, the winners being bicycle mechanics.

The key point, as you may have guessed, is that innovation requires both a clear problem definition and a value metric to determine what success looks like. Without these elements, your innovation efforts cannot be both successful and efficient. In other words, you may achieve success, but you will waste resources along the way. In the Lego case, rather than rely only on its own internal resources, Lego opened up its innovation efforts to external parties (customers) who were as well, or better, able to identify the problem to be solved than Lego's marketing and R&D team. As a "toy" company, Lego may have asked their constituents to offer up new products (what Lego might be solving for). Instead, Lego is asking for its customers to share what they are building and why it's fun. Customers understand that problem better than the company!

Incumbents are great at solving two types of problems: 1) how to extend existing capabilities and existing products (e.g., product line extensions) and 2) how to do what they already do more efficiently. As such, innovation inside incumbent firms is generally indexed very highly to these two problems. The outcome of this problem solving typically results in new products (e.g., Coke Life), hopefully generating revenue or process improvement, reducing cost, and freeing up capacity to do more. Insurgents, on the other hand, are generally better at solving two different problems: 1) how to solve specific problems for customers (at the expense of the incumbent) and 2) building alternative business models governed by a different set of rules and assumptions (again at the expense of the incumbent). Insurgents are generally much better than incumbents in problem/value definition, being resource-constrained and therefore tightly focused and more nimble and agile. This can be a significant advantage to the insurgent over the incumbent. The incumbent however, having more resources available, often has the upper hand if its problem definition and focus are clear and its execution is fast enough to make a difference in the market.

I recall having a discussion with some friends about the rise of China's military relative to the United States. On one side of the argument, it was stated that the United States will remain dominant militarily for decades to come with spending that outpaces China by about 3:1. My argument was that the United States, as the incumbent, is so wrapped up in maintaining and extending its existing platforms and so risk-averse in the development of new programmes, and the programmes take so long, that the two were much closer to parity (on an incremental basis) than it seems on paper. China, being less risk-averse, nimbler and less burdened by the need to invest in legacy platforms, probably has parity with the United States in terms of output per dollar invested, particularly when factoring input costs and red tape. It needs only to develop platforms that frustrate American capability, e.g., find ways to disrupt carrier battle groups, fixed bases, or tank divisions. Also, China is able to "draft" American R&D, producing similar capabilities at a fraction of the cost. For example, the Chinese J-20 aircraft is reported to be less than 50% of the cost per unit of the American F-35 aircraft, both fifth-generation platforms (Huang, 2016). While we don't know what the development budget was for the J-20 platform, it can be assumed that it was a small fraction of that of the F-35.

In the corporate world, the same applies to IT development. A couple of smart coders in a garage can often run circles around incumbent IT departments and deliver the same, often superior, functionality at a fraction of the cost and time invested. Yet incumbents are unwilling or unable to use these same resources to develop their solutions, opting instead for their own industrial scale resources who tend to create gold-plated solutions at a glacial speed. This is an overstatement for most firms but not too far off for some.

If innovation is defined by the application of know-how to solve problems that create value, then it follows that innovation must then be further defined by the types of problems firms seek to solve. As such, the capabilities deployed to solve those problems must also be different. We find that there are five broad problem types that face organisations:

1. Development of new products and services
2. Improving efficiency and productivity of existing resources
3. Building new capabilities
4. Creating new experiences for/with customer customers
5. Creating new business models

Each of the above problems has a different set of value metrics and requires different methodologies and skill sets. In most cases, these problems will overlap. For example, new business models are seldom possible without new capabilities, but the opposite doesn't always apply. The above list can be read as if in priority order for incumbents, the majority of resources in the incumbent firm being deployed towards product development to fuel growth. This is closely followed by focus on streamlining and improving existing processes to deliver existing services better, faster, and cheaper. For the most part, these problems are internal to the firm. All of these problems are important to insurgents, but the emphasis is more balanced in favour of 1, 4, and 5 above.

Using the Insurgence X/Y framework (see Exhibit 28), we can characterise these five problems as five types of innovation, each representing one element of the framework:

1. Y-axis innovation, i.e., product and service innovation
2. "In the box" innovation, i.e., process innovation
3. Capability innovation
4. Customer frontier innovation
5. X-axis innovation, i.e., business model innovation

Therefore, there is no such thing as "innovation" in a general sense for most firms. These five innovation types can be viewed as part of an innovation

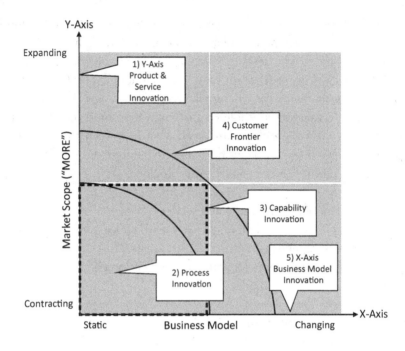

Exhibit 28 Innovation framework.

portfolio with different emphasis at different stages of a firm's lifecycle and are highly dependent on contextual stability. For example, an incumbent firm at a late stage of maturity in a stable market context will emphasise "in the box"/process innovation (to improve profitability) first, followed by Y-axis/ product innovation to create lifecycle extensions for existing products. This same firm, experiencing an unstable context, will need to prioritise X-axis/ business model innovation and customer frontier innovation to defend against (or initiate) disruption. Firms must build innovation capabilities to solve all five problem types and develop internal resources and external networks to ensure that they are well positioned to solve each problem type. Most incumbent firms have little or no customer frontier or business model innovation capabilities at least relative to the other innovation types.

For incumbents that have developed these capabilities, the bigger issue is the development of the leadership, culture, and agility required to translate innovation into results. This can be very challenging for incumbents that have never been required to think differently about their business models, customers, or capabilities and, typically, very few people inside incumbent organisations are able to see beyond existing products, processes, and customer relationships, often including senior leadership. Most business professionals at all levels, from our experience, are keen to innovate or be part of a firm that is innovative. The problem is 1) they don't know how, 2) there is often a lack of clear problem definition, 3) there is a tremendous amount of effort required to simply run in place, and 4) there are insufficient incentives. In the manufacturing company mentioned above, there was a very strong process innovation culture. People from across the business were well trained in continuous improvement techniques, were able to find problems to solve, and, in general, generated results. Unfortunately, many of their good ideas were not implemented, owing, in part, to the supply of new ideas being much greater than the available capacity to process them. Having put in the effort to create innovation ideas and not seeing follow through does not encourage employees to put their hand up the next time an idea comes along. Also, considering that across the board the business was solving the wrong problem at the wrong time, the innovation programme was viewed with a healthy degree of cynicism across the business. This same firm almost totally lacked any skills in customer frontier innovation, capability innovation, and business model innovation. All of their innovation for growth was driven by extracting more incremental value from existing products and services, most of which were mature or in decline.

The importance of culture in innovation cannot be understated. When clients ask me what the first step is to build this culture, I always give the same answer, "start with the customer". Because most incumbents are inward-looking, the first step on the path to building an innovation culture is to get the business to view itself objectively from the outside-in. For many reasons this can be challenging and uncomfortable, but I have never, not once, met an executive, or any employee, who had any trouble rallying around their customers once this became a shared rally point. This is especially helpful for firms that do not have an obvious burning platform as we saw with Lego. Progressively opening up the perspective of the business to the role of emerging trends and competition is also helpful to awaken people in the organisation *why* innovation is important. It cannot be abstract. Most incumbents know how to improve processes but are less comfortable with the application of other innovation methods. The second thing to focus on is motion. It is important that the business mobilises resources including budget and people to solve problems, *all the time*. This means that discretionary effort should be turned into projects designed to solve problems (as above). Leadership needs to provide clear direction regarding the problems to be solved and make available the resources to solve those problems, recognising and rewarding failures as much as successes so long as learnings are applied and mistakes are not repeated. Finally, metrics have to be established that materially differ from the operational metrics employed by the firm to maintain the core business. Innovation is about problem solving but inevitably leads to change. Reverting back to our Kodak example, in the early days of digital imaging, of course the margins were lower, and the projects were unprofitable. It is entirely unreasonable to expect otherwise. Many incumbents kill innovation right out of the gate by holding projects to inappropriate metrics and risk profiles. Insurgents are, again, unburdened by these issues because they are comfortable with risk and ambiguity in a way that incumbents are not. The only way to build a successful culture of innovation in an incumbent is to break down these orthodoxies. While I have focused here on the five major problem types and the corresponding innovation types, a strong argument can be made that innovation can be applied to culture and organisation as much as process, customer, and product.

Unfortunately, the market is very fragmented when it comes to innovation. The number of resources available are legion and cutting through the noise is very difficult. There are literally thousands of resources available to support each of the five innovation domains described above as well as numerous perspectives on innovation types. Starting with the customer, the methods we find most useful to support customer innovation are: 1) design thinking, 2) experience co-creation (Prahalad, 2004), 3) ethnography, and 4) journey mapping (subject to above comments). For product and service innovation: 1) the Lean start-Up approach mentioned above (Ries, 2011) and 2) Product and Cycle Time Excellence (PACE) (McGrath, 2004). For business model innovation: 1) Business Model Generation (note: we do not find the business model canvas concept to be particularly useful in business model design but very useful to describe existing business models) and 2) MIT model on business model archetypes (Weill et al., 2005). For process innovation: 1) Lean Six Sigma and 2) the New Manufacturing Challenge (Suzaki, 1987). Finally, for capability innovation: 1) Capability Mapping (described above) and 2) Blue Ocean Strategy (Kim and Mauborgne, 2015).

When it comes to ideation, we find that techniques that help would-be innovators to extend know-how to be very helpful. One of the most effective methods is to apply analogues to each of the problem types mentioned above. For example, if trying to discover how to build the first airplane, it would be logical to develop an understanding of how birds fly. In business, especially for incumbents, the ability of leaders and managers to "break out of the box" is often limited. As such the application of analogues can also be helpful. Have a logistics problem? Consider how Amazon would solve the problem. An analogue is something that is similar or comparable but not so close as to be the same. One innovator I met once told me, "If you asked me to build a new kind of bus shelter, the last thing I would do would be to look at other bus shelters for inspiration". Working in the opposite direction we find that "assumption busting" can also be a particularly useful technique. For example, UBER would not be possible (in many places) without breaking down relatively fixed assumptions about taxi regulation, i.e., "what would the market look like if there was no taxi regulation?" Answer: Everyone would be a taxi driver. Sure enough, that's what UBER is, a company that enables anyone to be a "taxi" driver.

In summary, as leaders, we need to always focus our limited resources on the things that matter most. Innovation is no different. Therefore, our preference is to focus energy on very clear problems, apply the right innovation methodology and the right people to address the right problem type, and apply maximum force and speed to get to a solution. Once the problem is defined, tools such as crowdsourcing can be applied to open up additional perspectives inside and outside the enterprise. The X prize foundation provides a great model for this (see https://www.xprize.org/). Clear and present problems/opportunities that benefit society are identified and incentives created for literally anyone to contribute to their solutions. The key to success is in the clarity of problem definition. For example, at the time of writing there is a $20 million X prize to solve the problem of converting CO_2 from power plants into useful and valuable products (see https://www.xprize.org/prizes/carbon). We are not supportive of "let a thousand flowers bloom", unstructured, and undefined innovation and believe that this can create more damage than good. Innovation across the five disciplines described above must be managed as a portfolio. At any given time, any business will have some measure of all types of innovation, but the ratio of effort and focus will be different. Finally, there are very few one-size-fits-all innovation resources. For example, process innovation people are not typically well-suited to customer frontier innovation and vice versa.

References

Huang, K, 2016, America's F-35 fighter jet vs China's J-20: which is better, cheaper, stealthier, *South China Morning Post*, viewed 21 August 2019, www.scmp.com/news/china/diplomacy-defence/article/2054492/americas-f-35-fighter-jet-vs-chinas-j-20-which-better.

Kim, WC & Mauborgne, R, 2015, *Blue Ocean Strategy, Expanded Edition: How to Create Uncontested Market Space and Make the Competition Irrelevant.* Harvard Business Review Press.

McGrath, ME, 2004, *Next Generation Product Development: How to Increase Productivity, Cut Costs, and Reduce Cycle Times.* McGraw-Hill, New York.

Prahalad, CK & Ramaswamy, V, 2004, *The Future of Competition – Co-Creating Unique Value with Customers.* Harvard Business Review Press, Boston, Massachusetts.

Ries, E, 2011, *The Lean Startup: How Today's Entrepreneurs Use Continuous Innovation to Create Radically Successful Businesses.* Crown Publishing Group.

Suzaki, K, 1987, *The New Manufacturing Challenge: Techniques for Continuous Improvement.* Free Press, New York.

Xprize.org, viewed 21 August 2019, https://www.xprize.org/.

Weill, Peter, Malone, Thomas W., D'Urso, Victoria T., Herman, George & Woerner, Stephanie, 2005, *Do Some Business Models Perform Better Than Others? A Study of the 1000 Largest US Firms.* MIT Sloan, http://ccs.mit.edu/papers/pdf/wp226.pdf

12 Implications for leadership

One of the biggest challenges faced by incumbents is leadership that is unable to effectively steer the firm through disruption. Perhaps more than anything else, leadership defines the difference between incumbents and insurgents. Can incumbent leaders become insurgent leaders having woken up to an imminent threat of disruption? Before we tackle this question, it is worth exploring what incumbent leadership looks like and how it is different from insurgent leadership.

Incumbent leadership

The only way to become an incumbent, other than to "buy your way in" with daddy's money, is by achieving some measure of success over time, building, growing, and expanding. The firm creates a model and a value proposition that customers respond to and then works hard to perfect and scale that model over time. As the firm grows and evolves more and more, functional specialisation is required to manage the complexity of the business. Choices need to be made regarding which markets to pursue, which products to emphasise, etc.; functional and business unit managers are hired each to contribute to their part of the whole. Senior leadership sets the vision, i.e., "we are going to be the #1 widget maker in our industry", and communicates that vision to everyone, getting their buy-in to the "cause". The business gets bigger and more functional. Metrics get established to communicate what is important ("more growth, less cost!"). The leaders inspire people to do great work (sell more film!) with authenticity and integrity. They make decisions and hold people accountable for their actions. They communicate and empower people to get things done to bring everyone on the journey. So far so good.

The dominant model of leadership and management in most incumbent firms (public, NFP, government, etc.) is based on military style command and control industrial model that replaced the craft guild model during the industrial revolution and that was cemented in place following the world wars of the 20th century, where our fathers, grandfathers, and great grandfathers (and no small number of mothers and grandmothers too!) came back from the wars into business and applying what they learned there to organisational management. During this time, owing to a number of factors, including slow communications, change happened relatively slowly. Their legacy is the "traditional" hierarchy with the leader (CEO) at the top, functional management in the middle, and workers (soldiers) at the bottom each with a set of specialist skills to perform a defined set of tasks. This works particularly well for large and complex organisations in highly stable contexts and is both efficient and prevents outright chaos. Power and influence in a command and control hierarchy is vertical and top-down. The CEO sets the vision, decides the strategy, and "cascades" that strategy from the top-down.

Over time, as the business matures, the hierarchy "hardens" and roles become silos and functions become like tribes, part of a whole but very protective of their turf. Each has a set of metrics that define exactly what is expected and managers optimise their priorities according to these metrics to unlock their incentive pay. In their wonderful article, "Understanding New Power", Jeremy Heimans and Henry Timms (2014) describe this type of power as "old power" and use the analogy of currency to describe how power is shared, hoarded, and spent in command and control organisations. Leadership power (knowledge, favour, praise, etc.) works hand in hand with budgetary power whereby leaders deploy resources top to bottom as well, funding projects that interest them, often based on the interests and wants of the most powerful leaders, then cascaded down to the next level and so on down the line. This all works very well when things are stable; when the major choices that leaders need to make are fundamentally Y-axis and "in the box" choices but breaks down in times of unstable context.

New leaders enter into incumbent firms with two major unwritten rules, the first being that the business model shall be fixed and the second is that the hierarchy must be preserved. These rules are quite invisible and reinforced by a power structure, culture, incentives, tribal loyalties, and a dozen other factors. The one rule that *is* written is that the leader must motivate the organisation to achieve "more". When context changes, requiring the firm to pivot, the amount of built-in resistance to change is incredibly strong and the battles to be fought to drive change through these obstacles are very difficult. As such, incumbent leaders tend to be incredibly risk-averse for fear of losing power or position. Too much change and the management team will revolt, or the board will fire the leader. Not enough change and, again, the leader will be fired. This is especially true of internally promoted CEOs, e.g., Mark Fields of Ford, who, having played a key role in getting the business to where it was pre-disruption, are less likely to initiate radical change. All of these factors add up to a leadership environment that has very low perceived degrees of freedom to act and an organisation with a very strong "invisible will" to maintain the status quo. According to Harvard (Marcec, 2018), the average tenure for large cap CEOs was 7.2 years in 2017, a relatively long time in consideration of the speed of change experienced today by most firms. A cynic might argue that long tenures equate to "cooking time" to further harden the incumbent's position. An optimist might argue that it takes two years to understand the problem, two years to solve the problem and three years to harvest the benefits. Whichever way you look at it, change is too slow in large incumbent enterprises. When context changes and the positioning of an incumbent becomes unstable in the market, it can be very hard to adjust in time. In the Blockbuster case, the CEO knew what to do but was unable to get the change through the infighting and Board decision process, ultimately failing to move the dial on digital distribution.

Insurgent leadership

Insurgents are unburdened by most of these factors and, as mentioned above, exist to solve different problems using different assumptions whilst playing a different game, thus undermining many of the weaknesses of the incumbent. Insurgent leaders are not (too) risk-averse. They are able to operate in an environment of high uncertainty and risk and thrive under these conditions knowing that rewards will be enormous if successful and life will go on if not. Insurgent organisations, especially at early stages, are far more horizontal than vertical because insurgents exist not to protect and defend an existing product, model, or customer but to solve one problem after another in rapid succession, for example:

- How do I create viable products?
- How do I get my products to market?
- How do I create a scalable business model?

- How do I avoid running out of cash?
- Can I meet payroll this month?

In order to do this, insurgent leaders are masters of assembling the best talent available to them, throwing them at a problem to be solved, solving it, and then moving on to a new problem, often with completely different talent deployed to solve the problem. As such, insurgent leaders are masters of "David" as in David and Goliath. It's easy to motivate the right kind of people with an underdog story and even easier to sequence solving the problem, i.e., "killing Goliath", into a defined set of problems to be solved one after another. Insurgent leaders are not particularly precious where their resources come from and are able to call upon talent from both inside and outside the firm as and when needed. This is what we mean by horizontal leadership. The problem to be solved, not the hierarchy and functional specialisation, dictates the skills required.

The definition of the endpoint (kill Goliath), clarification of the problem to be solved ("build an accurate sling to hit Goliath with"), and the assembly of talent to solve each problem (sling grip, length of string, type and weight of projectile, etc.) are all key to the insurgent leader's success. This requires insurgent leaders to place a much higher value on "frictionless cooperation of multidisciplinary resources" than "positional authority of specialised resources". The insurgent model of iterating talent against well-defined problems is much more project-based and much less focused on repetitive tasks, at least until the insurgent reaches scale, at which time functionalisation and specialisation become more and more gravitational. Insurgent leaders view resources differently than incumbents, often managing them like a day trader manages equities (churn and burn). Insurgent leaders sometimes so constantly redeploy resources and talent and at such a pace that makes outsiders (and some employees) downright angry and burn out is quite common in these firms. Resources are along for the ride as long as they can contribute, not a moment longer. All of this adds up to an incredibly fast-paced mode of leadership.

Elon Musk typifies the insurgent approach in his leadership of Space X, an aerospace firm. His bold vision of bringing humans to Mars provides a "kill Goliath" backdrop that is hard to imagine being anything less than inspiring to employees. Yet this big vision is broken down into an incredibly granular series of problems to be solved, some technical (reusable rocketry), some political (get NASA to fund some of their effort), some competitive (dislodge

United Launch Alliance from existing government contracts). Space X is working at a very high velocity and has gone from a standing start just over a decade ago to the dominant player globally (by share of new commercial launches) (Sheetz, 2018). Musk encourages his leaders to hire people based on "passion, drive, and talent" and "hiring people better than themselves", according to vice president of human resources, Brian Bjelde (Moore, 2017) in a 2017 Glassdoor interview.

As a leader, he also reportedly sees his role as one of enablement rather than control. This is the essence of the insurgent leader, define a big problem to solve, break it up into smaller problems, and assemble the best talent to get it done with incredible urgency.

Incumbent leaders tend to do the opposite. Somehow "beating last quarter" is just not as motivating as "getting to Mars". Also, modern leadership dogma suggests that leaders have to "bring everyone along on the journey". Some incumbent leaders take this too seriously and to mean that the "same team that got us to where we are today will be the team that takes us into the future". From my own experience as a member of a CEO peer group for 15 years, I can report that the #1 issue by far faced by most CEOs is their inability to make senior staff changes when required for routine reasons let alone to address disruptive change. A combination of guilt, feeling of failure, and genuine care for the well-being of their people often gets in the way of refreshing talent as a business evolves. Insurgents often care about the mission more than the employment tenure of a particular employee but that doesn't mean that they don't care about the person. Few people in their careers are able to participate in a team that is fundamentally changing the world. That counts for a lot even when sometimes clocking up the 99th hour at work in a week. We are not suggesting that people be treated like commodities but see the model of fixed long-term employment becoming increasingly obsolete as the assembly of talent to address an ever-increasing and diverse set of problems requires far more flexible models of deploying resources.

Bringing insurgent leadership to the incumbent

Can an insurgent leader succeed in an incumbent environment? At Microsoft, the answer seems to be an emphatic yes. In 2014, Satya Nadella, formerly the EVP of Microsoft's Cloud and Enterprise Group, became CEO. Microsoft, a long-term incumbent in a relatively new industry, was famous for Windows, its nearly ubiquitous operating system, its culture of management patronage (old power personified in a firm), and its fortress-like mentality (inability to play nicely with others in the market). Yet the business was successful – at the time of the leadership transition, one of the most valuable companies in the world (though behind Apple). In the years preceding Mr. Nadella, Microsoft was a decidedly Y-axis competitor with a mandate to extend Windows and Office products to every desktop globally. The business was fiercely competitive and insular, e.g., "down specifying" Microsoft Office for Apple Mac and refusing to make Office available on Apple tablet devices. Similarly, the company viewed Linux, the open-source operating system, as anathema and behaved accordingly in the marketplace. The business model for Microsoft Windows and Office products was an "on premise" licence model, whereby consumers and businesses would purchase licences for the software "in the box" having to buy new licences for significant new upgrades.

Microsoft, one of the great software companies of all time, missed the boat in social media and mobility and could not get past its Windows-centric mindset to build these capabilities. Famously, Microsoft purchased the Nokia consumer phone handset division in 2013, which was, even at that time, on the losing side of history up against Apple (iOS) and Google (Android). Microsoft was never able to achieve scale in either of these arenas and exited the business shortly thereafter.

At the time of the transition, Microsoft, like many incumbents, had increasingly lost touch with customers, becoming more and more of an inside-out firm. Windows 8 was poorly received by its customer base, a product that appeared to be developed by engineers without sufficient consideration to UX design, an "own goal" if there ever was one. As customer adoption of smartphones accelerated (tablets were just getting started), Microsoft alienated customers by not offering portability of the Microsoft core office suite to third-party platforms, instead focusing attention on developing an alternative Microsoft/Nokia ecosystem. As a firm starts to lose ground with customers, employees soon follow. This becomes a vicious cycle, and Microsoft was no exception.

The recipe for the turnaround followed many insurgent principles (The Economist, 2019):

- **Start with the customer** – i.e., fix what's wrong with the products and emphasise the experience and build products that create excitement (e.g., Microsoft Surface)

- **Get the team excited about the customer and growth** – happy, motivated employees lead to happy customers, results will follow
- **Open-up** – like LEGO, Mr. Nadella ended the closed shop mindset at Microsoft and opened up the products to third-party platforms, recognising that the risk of not participating was much greater than the risk of self-cannibalisation
- **Focus on the X-axis** – under Mr. Nadella's leadership, Office 365, a subscription "cloud-based" model, was scaled to replace the traditional on-premise business model, giving users continuous updates for a fixed fee. Microsoft also encouraged growth of Azure, its on-demand cloud computing service with an open mindset to Linux, as a key growth driver up against Amazon Web Services
- **Encourage risk taking and innovation** – perhaps more than anything, Mr. Nadella reprogrammed the Microsoft culture to take risks, drive growth, and learn from its mistakes
- **Abolish "soul destroying" stack ranking** – Microsoft's performance management system, based on forced ranking of employees from best to worst, created a culture of fear and resentment but also stifled innovation as employees were unwilling to take risks and end up on the bottom of the pile, a potential career killer. Forced ranking also created intense internal competition, knowledge and power hoarding, and "white anting" (i.e., active undermining of colleagues) (Buckingham, 2013). This process was replaced with a more humane system designed to encourage risk taking and collaboration at all levels.

My own experience with Microsoft as a customer has evolved over this time from intense dislike (one too many blue screens pushed me to embrace Apple), to plain dislike (I used to hate that the Office products on Apple products were inferior), to ambivalence (once they fixed this problem, I began to grudgingly like the Office products on the Mac), to curiosity (in 2018 I purchased a $7000.00 Surface Studio just because of the beautiful design), to a fan – the Office 365 experience is now so good it is almost a joy to use.

Microsoft is now reaping the rewards of this major transformation and is in a quarter-by-quarter duel with Apple over the crown of the "world's most valuable company". At the time of writing, Microsoft's market capitalisation is over $1 trillion.

Incumbent firms are steadily making the transition. Horizontal leadership and project-based problem solving is becoming more common as incumbent firms struggle to adjust to instability and disruption. Many incumbent firms have begun to reorganise work and the workplace around enablement of teams, understanding that bringing talent together to rapidly solve problems for customers is fast becoming the most important leadership capability required to enable sufficient agility in the marketplace. We believe that this leadership inversion, where leaders exist to support these teams and remove roadblocks and red tape as described above, will gradually replace command and control management systems particularly as the next generation of leaders displaces baby boomers and Generation X in senior management roles.

It's a good thing too. As the workforce transitions to the next generation of leadership, command and control will become increasingly obsolete as young people in the workforce demand different ways of working anchored by a strong sense of meaning (i.e., working on something important, aligned to their values, and interesting). Insurgents are well ahead of the curve on these ways of working having forged new leadership styles in garages, sheds, and incubators over the last two decades. Incumbents must embrace these principles in order to build resilience against disruption and, ultimately, make the transition from defence to offence. The business case for the change is easy to justify given the ongoing "war for talent" in the marketplace. Those firms that don't adapt on this dimension will find it difficult to secure critical resources or be stuck with an inferior workforce.

In our search for new thinking on incumbent vs. insurgent leadership, we came across a book, entitled "Why Nations Fail" by Daron Acemoglu and James Robinson (Acemoglu and Robinson, 2012). The main thesis of the book was that "inclusive" political and economic institutions have a much greater probability of long-term success (i.e., are superior) as compared to "extractive" political and economic institutions which are, ultimately, doomed to fail or languish. In the weeks following reading this book, I began to wonder about the role that this theory could play in describing organisations and how this fits our model of insurgence. Are organisations (and leaders) that practice extractive methods also doomed to fail? Are insurgents inherently better than incumbents at practising inclusive methods?

Like nations, organisations have political (organisational) and economic domains which must be optimised over time to ensure longevity and success. Much has been written about the need to balance the needs of multiple stakeholders to ensure the long-term sustainability of an organisation. Typically, this means that the interests of the company, the shareholder, the customer, and the employees are aligned. Increasingly, the community is included in this equation.

An "extractive organisation" could be described as an organisation that disproportionately favours one stakeholder group over another, most typically senior management and shareholders, at the expense of the others. For example, Sears Roebuck & Co. has been criticised as a company for overly focusing on short-term shareholder value at the expense of other stakeholders (e.g., "investing" free cash to buy back shares rather than investing in much needed infrastructure, advertising, and new retail concepts) (Isidore, 2018). These organisations are also typically extractive (i.e., pay lower wages, provide fewer incentives, etc.) in their leadership and employment practices and are more likely to have command and control management models. The cash hoarding of Western firms over the past decade indicates that many incumbent firms may be going backwards on this metric and becoming more extractive (Economist, 2016) and this is one explanation of the rising income gap in developed economies.

In contrast, an "inclusive organisation" tends to find a healthy balance between internal stakeholders (especially management and employees) and has an inclusive economic model, whereby benefit is shared more equally amongst employees, management, shareholders, customers, and the community. The cultures of inclusive organisations tend to be more merit-based and co-creative, with contributing individuals able to participate and share in the organisation's innovation agenda (and the fruit of this contribution). These organisations are usually more flexible and dynamic and better able to deploy resources where they count the most as well as to more easily make adjustments as conditions change.

We believe that extractive firms in *unstable markets* are, over the long run, more likely to fail and, in the short run, these organisations will be much more vulnerable to disruption. We also believe that, over time, incumbents tend to become more extractive, whereas insurgents tend to be more inclusive both organizationally and economically. For leaders, the important question becomes – "is your organisation extractive or inclusive?"

References

Acemoglu, D & Robinson, JA, 2012, *Why Nations Fail: The Origins of Power, Prosperity, and Poverty*. Profile Books, London.

Anon, 2016, Too much of a good thing: profits are too high. America needs a giant dose of competition, *The Economist*, viewed 25 August 2019, https://economist.com/briefing/2016/03/26/too-much-of-a-good-thing.

Anon, 2019, What Microsoft's revival can teach other tech companies, *The Economist*, viewed 22 August 2019, https://economist.com/leaders/2019/07/25/what-microsofts-revival-can-teach-other-tech-companies.

Buckingham, M, 2013, Trouble with the curve? Why Microsoft is ditching stack rankings, *Harvard Business Review*, viewed 25 September 2019, https://hbr.org/2013/11/dont-rate-your-employees-on-a-curve.

Heimans, J & Timms, H, 2014, Understanding "new power", *Harvard Business Review*, viewed 22 August 2019.

Isadore, C, 2018, How Sears wasted $6 billion that could have kept it out of bankruptcy, *CNN Business*, viewed 29 September 2019, https://edition.cnn.com/2018/10/30/business/sears-share-repurchase/index.html.

Marcec, D, 2018, CEO tenure rates, *Equilar, Inc.*, viewed 22 August 2019, https://corpgov.law.harvard.edu/2018/02/12/ceo-tenure-rates/.

Moore, E, 2017, Inside SpaceX: what it's like working for a company on a mission to Mars, viewed 22 August 2019, https://glassdoor.com/blog/spacex-best-places-to-work/.

Sheetz, M, 2018, How Elon Musk's rocket company SpaceX beat Boeing to become a $28 billion aerospace juggernaut, viewed 22 August 2019, www.cnbc.com/2018/05/22/spacex-leading-the-space-race-to-launch-humans-to-mars.html.

13 | Implications for strategy execution

Strategy Execution, aka "getting things done", is a perennial problem for executives in incumbent organisations. There are dozens of methods to choose from, each with advantages and disadvantages depending on external factors (e.g., context stability) and internal factors (e.g., the discipline of the leadership). In early 2019, Richard Bulsulwa, Bruce Gurd, and I presented research on this topic, and many of the methods in mainstream use, in our book, "Strategy Execution and Complexity: Thriving in the Era of Disruption" (Busulwa, Tice, and Gurd, 2018) with a central thesis of the book focused on *ambidexterity*, i.e., the simultaneous pursuit of internal efficiency and external market flexibility. As noted in the book, some methods are better suited than others for internal vs. external focus. One of my favourite works on the topic of strategy execution, "Strategy and the Fat Smoker: Doing What's Obvious but Not Easy", by David Maister (2008) sums it up nicely in the title. You are a fat smoker, and therefore unhealthy; it's obvious what you need to do (i.e., quit smoking and start exercising), but you are somehow unable to do it. It is an excellent analogy for incumbent strategy execution. This resonates particularly well considering my experience working with many incumbent organisations in this arena over more than 20 years.

Insurgents are again different. Strategy execution is not usually a concept that resonates for insurgents, the main reason that providers of strategy execution services often fail to find a market with start-ups. Why? It's simple. Every single activity pursued by the insurgent is, by definition, strategy execution. Insurgents have strategies just like incumbents do, but their attitude and mindset to execution of the strategy is not an additional activity on top of the core business, it is the core business. Insurgents exist in a state of what we describe as "hyper-mobilisation". Hyper-mobilisation is about placing maximum focus on something important (in this case, the strategy) and mobilising as many of the *right* resources as can be found to achieve an outcome as quickly as possible. Once the outcome is described and the goal is clear, the organisation is highly motivated to get it done through rapid cycles of experimentation and learning until the goal is achieved. Hyper-mobilisation is also about removing barriers and constraints that are in the way as quickly as possible and recognising that many constraints are artificial or internal and therefore easier to remove than others. Necessarily the tempo is high in hyper-mobilised organisations. You know them when you see them. The Apollo program was a case study in hyper-mobilisation, with literally hundreds of thousands of people feverishly working towards a common goal, on an absurdly aggressive timeline, to achieve something that has never been done before. As I write this, it is now the 50th anniversary of Apollo. When it comes to manned spaceflight since Apollo, NASA has been anything but hyper-mobilised, lacking clear and consistent political direction and the resources to make anything happen (in terms of human space exploration at least) other than at a snail's pace. It is almost an embarrassment that America lacks the capability to place a human being in orbit without Russian support.

Space X, mentioned in the previous chapter, is hyper-mobilised. The entire SpaceX team is directed at the goal of getting humans off the planet and into space. The company, in spite of its success with the Falcon 9, a platform that is now almost virtually unchallenged in commercial space flight, the business is working at an almost furious pace to replace the platform with something better. Its competitors, over the entire life of SpaceX, have been unable to bring a single new platform to the market in the same time that SpaceX has developed five variants of the Falcon 9, the Falcon Heavy, and now soon the "Starship". Anyone who doubts the possibility of hyper-mobilisation at scale need only look at Apollo or the Manhattan Project. Anyone who thinks that those are unfair examples, owing to the ludicrous amount of budget and resources these programs had, need only look at SpaceX. There are five key principles to hyper-mobilisation:

1. A *clear and unambiguous goal* shared by all people involved in achieving that goal (please note that the goal may be big or small and represent the solving of a problem as much as achieving something new)
2. Total dedication and deployment of the *right resources* to achieve the goal, regardless of where the resources come from

3. Total dedication to a *FAST* "try-fail-learn-implement-scale-repeat" cycle. Every setback is a learning opportunity

4. Total leadership dedication to *removal of constraints*, barriers, red tape, and other hindrances that prevent the goal from being achieved

5. A culture absolutely *dedicated to success and winning* (see below) and imbued with a deep belief that success is not only possible but inevitable

Insurgents, as mentioned in the previous chapter, assemble their resources horizontally, directed like an arrow at a target. Vertical hierarchies are the enemy of hyper-mobilisation. Power, positioning, agendas, siloed capability, and many other things get in the way of hyper-mobilisation. Leaders in vertically oriented firms wish to monitor progress, not necessarily getting their hands dirty in the trenches removing obstacles. Incumbents are usually very poor at hyper-mobilisation except in times of crisis.

I recall in my role as a nuclear engineer with the US Navy being asked, at a very young age, to participate on the Executive Committee of a Naval Shipyard (with the implicit understanding that I would mostly keep my mouth shut) as part of the quality program. We met in a boardroom overlooking the river, with a very nice view of city. There was a major problem to be solved on one of our programs and we debated the problem in every monthly meeting over the course of about 6 months, each time leaving the problem unresolved with a promise of further analysis between meetings to find an answer to the problem. As I sat there listening to these men debate the problem, often rehashing the same points, I frequently tuned out of the discussion, instead looking out the window at the construction, from the ground up, of a brand-new baseball stadium across the river. It was finished at about the time of our sixth meeting, by which time the problem we were trying to solve had become a standing agenda item and, increasingly, a critical path issue. Somewhere during that sixth monthly meeting, I lost my patience and broke the above implicit rule ("keep your mouth shut kid") and, having no further interest in hearing these guys discuss this problem any further, I directed everyone to look out the window and observe the stadium. A few of the people in that meeting seemed only to acknowledge the stadium for the first time. The universal response of the team in that meeting was, with very angry stares, "who let this kid into this meeting?" and "where the hell did that stadium come from?" My point was simple. In the time we wasted debating a single problem, some group of *civil* engineers across the river built an entire stadium! On a roll, and figuring I would be fired anyway, I went as far as to suggest that we were very poor engineers by comparison, having not been able to solve this problem in *six* months. On the theory that "no good deed goes unpunished", the chairman asked me how I would solve the problem. My answer was simple. We are not leaving this room until the problem is resolved. We are going to solve it NOW. And we did. We pulled three senior engineers from three departments out of their offices and into the room along with several chiefs (the right resources) and worked the problem until it was solved. After that, we applied the same approach to every meeting, seeking important problems to solve that prevented the "business" from getting things done and applying the right resources to solve them. We began to *mobilise*.

Most incumbents can tell tales that sound very much like the first part of my story, not the second. Entrepreneurs think the story is foolish. Of course, you work the problem to resolution as quickly as practicable. This contrast between incumbents and insurgents, perhaps more than anything else, describes why disruption can happen so quickly. It takes a relatively long time for an insurgent to gain momentum in the market but once that momentum is there – bam – the insurgent displaces the incumbent. For example, while the team at United Launch Alliance (ULA) is cautiously ramping up its Vulcan rocket program, SpaceX is already testing its next generation of rockets in the field.

Can incumbents hyper-mobilise?

To be sure, the deck is stacked against you as an incumbent to be able to hyper-mobilise. It is difficult to assemble talent across organisational boundaries and to enlist their discretionary effort (i.e., the amount of time available after all of the "day job" activities are completed) towards any objective quickly. Add in all of the other pressures pushing against hyper-mobilisation, it can be very difficult indeed. For example:

- No incentives to participate in these teams other than good corporate citizenship
- Metrics that keep people in the orbit of the day job, not the night job
- The "need" to collect more and more data to make decisions
- Lack of clarity on who will "own" the program of work (in other words, who to blame if it fails)
- Too many other competing priorities

- Need for speed is abstract – no obvious lion chasing you to get things done
- Need to write a "paper" and wait for the board to get the item on their agenda
- Don't control all of the necessary resources to get things done
- Systems are not compatible with the change
- Lack of funding or other resources
- Too risk-averse – unwilling to experiment with solutions for fear of failure

I could literally fill the rest of the book with reasons that incumbents are unable to hyper-mobilise, but I think you see the point. When I see this list, I am encouraged that hyper-mobilisation is possible for incumbents. Why? Simply because each of these items falls within the control of the firm. Anything that can be controlled can be changed. Hard work? Yes. Impossible? No. Don't control the resources? Get them from outside. Too many competing priorities? Reprioritise your work. Wrong metrics? Change them. Lack buy-in? Go out and get it.

The things, in my experience, that motivate people more than anything else are success, motion, and meaning in that order. Unfortunately, one has to nurture motivation in the opposite order, i.e., meaning, motion, and success. Meaning comes from a clear goal or problem to be solved and an alignment of the needs of the individual or team with the needs of the firm. Meaning, above all, comes from a congruence of an individual's goals, mindset, and values with the firms. Finding meaning requires empathy and clarity from the outset. Investment in time in establishing this congruence comes from a clear definition of the goal/problem/opportunity and an understanding of "what's in it for me" (WIFM) is important and seldom a waste of time.

Motion comes from making a determined effort to be in a state of mobilisation at all times, i.e., "fast and furious", and success starts as a belief (we can succeed) and then develops into a confidence (we are actually doing it!). These are all choices. Make them.

Often, we are asked the question by incumbents, "my strategy isn't working, why?" Insurgents almost never ask this question as they know their strategy isn't working at any precise moment in time but are iterating like crazy to get the strategy to work and scale. They are comfortable with failure and learning in a way that incumbents are not. The rocket blew up? Great!!! What did we learn from it?

What follows is a sometimes tongue-and-cheek viewpoint on why, from the author's experience, incumbents fail to execute strategy along with some examples to illustrate. It should be noted that these reasons, framed as the "big five", are often concurrent.

Reason #1: you suck at your core business!

While this sounds like it may be a joke, it isn't. Many incumbent businesses are inferior but don't know it. They have an internal belief that they are GREAT. After all, customers buy their services, associations give them awards, employees love working there. As I mentioned many times, incumbents tend to look inward, not outward. Success is almost always relative and positional with regard to customers and competition. I once gave a talk to a group of chief executives about strategy and disruption and at the beginning of the meeting I asked each of them how their business was going. One CEO was particularly ebullient about the performance of his business, having posted 8% growth on the previous year. Everyone else in the room was more bearish about their performance, none growing faster than 8% (it was a room full of incumbents). He was particularly worried about disruption in his industry (it was a real estate business), this being the topic of discussion. In particular, he felt that the business was largely unsuccessful in pursuing new initiatives that would help him future proof the business. At one point in the discussion, I made the "inside-out, out-side in point" and I noticed that for the next 90 minutes he was tuned out of the discussion. Eventually, I checked in with him and he related something very interesting. While his business was growing at 8%, and he felt great about that, the rest of his industry peers were growing at nearly double that rate! "Discovering" the idea that his business was growing more slowly than the market was a sobering insight for this leader (it was a $50 million business). His business, at best, was rising like a boat on the tide and, at worst, slowly drifting out to sea. His conclusion, "how can I expect my change initiatives to succeed when we are losing ground in our core business – we *suck* at our core business and don't even know it". Yahoo comes to mind as an example of this. Once a great (and big) business, now a footnote, Yahoo, other than making some wise investments, was not sufficient to the task of beating Google in search and therefore was not able to sustain a large share of ad revenues.

Reason #2: you have the wrong strategy

This happens much more often than one might think. Many strategies fail in the execution because the strategy itself is not well aligned to market trends or isn't a strategy so much as a business doing more of what it already does, more often and in more places. In Chapter 4, we described Masters Hardware failing to get a toehold and build scale in the Australian retail hardware market based on flawed assumptions leading to a strategy that was fundamentally incompatible with the market conditions, competition, and consumer needs. The same thing happened with the Microsoft/Nokia acquisition. The world did not need another mobile application ecosystem. Bad execution often follows bad strategy. Often leaders blame the execution.

One company we worked with was losing share to its competition and gradually eroding its profitability each quarter. Just as the CEO was retiring, we were asked to comment on the performance of the business by the incoming CEO to help him get in tune with the issues in the business. As part of this process we met with each executive, asking questions about the business and why it was failing to meet expectations. The outgoing CEO placed the problem squarely in the execution camp feeling that his strategy was very strong but that his team was letting him down in the execution (you can begin to see one problem already). The business, a second-tier rental car company, was seeking to match the market leader at that time in terms of price and fleet options, investing millions of dollars in new information technology to enable its systems to adapt to new fleet options and to autonomously monitor the competition's pricing. The value proposition of the firm was based on offering a price discount to the leader in the market but also matching the leader in the market on fleet, service, and locations. It was suggested that the leadership team come together to discuss the problem together and see if a solution to the firm's execution problem be discovered and addressed. The leading solution theory was "fire and replace the CIO". Morale was poor owing to the business not winning and an almost universal frustration with the poor execution.

The meeting was difficult and quickly developed into a gang-up on the CIO to the extent that one executive actually tossed a shoe at him during the meeting. The consensus amongst the team was that, without the IT upgrades, the business would continue to slide in performance. The incoming CEO took a different view on the situation. His take was that matching the market leader across the board on everything except price would make the problem worse, not better. In fact, he felt that acceleration of the IT program would enable a strategy that would put the company at serious risk, particularly in light of incoming competition from ride-share and Uber. When asked to answer the question, "what is the key to the market leader's success in the market?" the answer was obvious but, *having never been asked*, elusive to the team. As it turns out, all things equal *scale* was the key to the market leader's cost leadership position. This company, a fraction of the size of the largest player in the market, built a strategy around beating the *cost leader* in the market on *price*. Once this insight emerged, it became clear that not only was the implementation of the systems project not the problem, it might even make it worse! They had the wrong strategy and yet blamed the performance problem on the execution, and the execution of the IT program in particular. The leadership then pursued other options that were a better fit in consideration of the market, the customer, and the competition.

Reason #3: your business is subject to disruption

While disruption is not necessarily the main topic of this book, the assumption of disruption is a key part of the tale of incumbents and insurgents. The old saw, Q: "how did you bankrupt?" A: "two ways, first gradually, then suddenly" (Hemingway, 1926), often holds true. In this book, we have placed a great deal of emphasis on solving the right problem. Incumbents often solve the wrong problem and thus even effective execution can accelerate the demise of the business. This is a variation on the "wrong strategy" theme to be sure. As we have discovered, disruption is, more often than not, driven by competition on the X-axis, not the Y-axis. The fatal mistake of the incumbent victim of disruption is to execute a Y-axis strategy against an X-axis opponent.

Kodak's introduction of the Advantix film platform, the Kodak name for the Advanced Photo System, is a great example. Introduced in the mid-1990s, Advantix was a line extension of film for consumer use (and to a lesser degree, professional use) in the early years of digital cameras coming into the market. The product was designed as a cartridge that could be snapped into a film camera without feeding the film tab into the camera (some readers will have never experienced this) and the format was designed to capture some additional information such as date and time of the photo (i.e., metadata about the photograph). This product, on the eve of the disruption of film by digital imaging, was a not a success in spite of an estimated $500 million program to plan, launch, and market the product. While the product execution was a success in terms of getting the product to market, unfortunately for Kodak the product was irrelevant almost as soon as it launched (Mui, 2012).

While Kodak executed Advantix perfectly but was still disrupted, Nokia, the first mover in smartphone technology, was too slow to respond to faster rivals Apple and Google, each company hyper-mobilised in a race to dominate the market for smartphone OS. Apple's app store and associated ecosystem alongside Google's Android platform and associated ecosystem, each X-axis disruptions, created the death blow to Nokia, defending its own mobile operating system, Symbian. Nokia was unable to adjust quickly enough, presumably partly because of a fear of cannibalisation of their handset install base and the Nokia OS. In 10 years, from 2003 to 2013, Nokia went from undisputed market leader to exit, selling to Microsoft in 2013. By all accounts, the business was hamstrung by internal politics and fear of change effectively paralysing the efforts of Nokia to execute its digital strategy (Change, 2012).

Reason #4: you lack execution discipline

As Richard, Bruce, and I discovered in the research leading up to our book on strategy execution in 2019, the majority of strategy execution methodologies are silent on reasons 1–3 above. The dominant assumption underpinning most strategy execution methodologies is what I call the "going concern" principle, i.e., the business is fundamentally healthy, and the strategy is, for the most part, correct. As we have seen, this is an unsafe assumption for any business in an unstable market context. That said, execution discipline is exactly what it sounds like, the discipline of getting the right (strategic) things done. Too much has been written on this topic already for me to re-tread various methodologies available. Rather, I will illustrate the key ingredients central to execution success and contrast each of these ingredients on the incumbent/insurgent spectrum.

I often ask business leaders, particularly middle-senior executives, to share their thoughts on the key ingredients to execution discipline. Not surprisingly, there is little debate as to *what* the ingredients are but much debate on *how* to bring these ingredients to life. Table 5 provides a summary of some of the more important ingredients.

Table 5 Execution Discipline Contrast: Incumbents and Insurgents

Ingredient	Incumbent	Insurgent
Vision	Broad platitudes, e.g., "be the #1 player in our industry"	Aimed at solving a specific problem or exploiting a specific opportunity
Objectives	Many, diverse, unfocused	Few, highly focused
Metrics	Short-term focus, favour the core business, inward focus	Short- and long-term focus on customers, growth, and scale, outward focus
Resource allocation	Allocate available resources in line with the annual budget	Allocate the best resources dynamically to solve the right problems
Alignment	Inside-out, cascading from top-down (i.e., sell the vision)	Outside-in (i.e., solve problems for the customer), assemble the right resources, manage horizontally
Mobilisation rate	Slow	Hyper fast
Governance	Top-down, vertical, slow and static, annual	Horizontal, continuous and dynamic, real time
Budget process	Leads the strategy process	Follows the strategy process
Planning	Slow and ponderous, objective-focused, compliance-driven	Lean, emergent, problem-focused, value-seeking
Initiatives	Too many, unfocused	Very few, highly focused
Risk	Risk-averse, driven by "hurdles"	Risk-tolerant, driven by data
Change management	Periodic thaw/freeze cycles	Continuous flux – way of life
Communications	Slow, episodic, and "official"/top-down	Real time and continuous
Constraints	Internal	External
Incentives	Favour the core business and short-term results (backward-looking)	Favours getting things done and improving leading indicators of long-term results (forward-looking)

It should be noted that all of these ingredients are viewed differently by insurgents. It is no surprise therefore that insurgents are less structured, more emergent, and much faster in their execution efforts. Being fair to incumbents, size is also a factor and large ships are indeed harder to turn than small ones. As we saw with large and complex firms like Microsoft, Amazon, and SpaceX, this is a thin excuse for slow and ponderous execution.

Reason #5: if it isn't 1–4, it's *you*

If your business is unable to get traction with your strategy, and it isn't definitively one of the above reasons, it's almost certainly a leadership failure. Incumbent leaders have different qualities from insurgent leaders as we have seen above in Chapter 12. Leadership is contextual. The captain of a ship who is used to operating in calm seas is often unprepared for a cyclone. The opposite also applies, a business that is used to operating on the edge of the abyss will have leaders who fall bored in stable times. Leadership refresh is very healthy. Unfortunately, top leadership comes with a healthy dose of ego and self-importance as well as big monetary rewards. It is very difficult for leaders to look in the mirror and admit that they are not well-suited for a new phase of a firm's life and give up all of the trappings and social standing associated with their position. As such, they often have to be removed rather than step aside gracefully. This need not be the case. I have met many business owners in small-to-medium businesses who have moved aside in favour of new management as conditions changed and still retained ownership and involvement, often in a sales or marketing role.

References

Busulwa, R, Tice, M & Gurd, B, 2018, *Strategy Execution and Complexity: Thriving in the Era of Disruption*. Routledge, Abingdon.

Chang, A, 2012, 5 reasons why Nokia lost its handset sales lead and got downgraded to 'Junk', *Wired*, viewed 22 August 2019, https://wired.com/2012/04/5-reasons-why-nokia-lost-its-handset-sales-lead-and-got-downgraded-to-junk/.

Hemingway, Ernest, 1926 (2006), *The Sun Also Rises*. Scribner, New York.

Maister, D, 2008, *Strategy and the Fat Smoker: Doing What's Obvious but Not Easy*. The Spangle Press, Boston, Massachusetts.

Mui, C, 2012, How Kodak failed, *Forbes*, viewed 22 August 2019, https://forbes.com/sites/chunkamui/2012/01/18/how-kodak-failed/#4f8cbd46f27a.

14 | **Eight principles of insurgence**

Having explored the differences between incumbents and insurgents through-out this book, the question *"how* can an incumbent learn to operate like an insurgent" remains to be answered. It is our strong belief that incumbents have significant advantages over insurgents in stable market conditions owing to a variety of factors including, brand, scale, ability to influence regulators and policy makers, etc. This advantage begins to rapidly erode when instabil-ity increases, thus undermining the incumbent advantage and opening up opportunities for would-be insurgents to attack the position of incumbents. In most cases, but not always, technology plays a role in creating instability, but we try not to overemphasise the role of technology in driving disruption (i.e., "digital disruption"), instead placing emphasis on the X-axis dynamics driving disruption and the role of alternative business models and assump-tions in driving disruption. Incumbents have the same access to technology as insurgents and superior resources to exploit technology, yet in many cases they are not able to harness these resources effectively.

What follows are eight principles of insurgence along with some advice for incumbent leaders to make smarter choices to help avoid falling into the "incumbent trap", i.e., self-inflicted inability to change. Most business models are not robust to contextual change in the long run. An understanding of this fact is a critical background point that leaders must understand. In other words, in the long run your business model *will* be disrupted, the only ques-tion is *when*. In almost every case of disruption we studied, the incumbent was aware of incipient disruption but was either unable to adjust owing to internal factors or significantly discounted the speed or the impact of the change. This need not be the case. Our preference is for healthy incum-bents to *initiate* disruption, not stand back and wait for it to wash over them.

In other words, play offence not defence. Each of the principles below are described in detail in the preceding chapters and summarised here with an implementation focus. It should be noted that these are cumulative and not discrete principles.

Principle 1: outside-in orientation

Perhaps more than anything else, an outside-in orientation is critical for incumbents to set the stage for insurgence. As discussed in previous chapters, the default position for incumbents is to focus inside, not outside, the firm. At some point in the evolution of the firm, the balance tips and the firm becomes ever more insular and defensive. Unless some major external threat emerges, this orientation is likely to continue, magnify, and solidify. Sometimes, even despite a clear external threat, incumbents prefer to retreat into themselves, focusing management energy and resources on taking costs out and restructuring without rethinking their business models or their core value propositions.

Making the shift from outside-in to inside-out starts with a recognition that a firm is not an island and exists only in the context of an interwoven ecosystem of competitors, customers, and other stakeholders. Inside-out firms typically project their own thinking onto the market and are woeful at recognising non-traditional, competitive threats that come from outside the industry "bubble" they operate in. The questions listed in Table 6 will help you identify your firm's internal/external orientation.

If the answers to the above questions are more aligned to the left side of Table 6, the orientation of your firm is more inside-out incumbent than outside-in insurgent. There are clues in each question regarding what to do to become more externally focused, but how? As with all change processes, the very first step is self-awareness and recognition. Generally speaking, a firm's inside-out orientation is not deliberate but rather a consequence of its evolution and success. When confronted with these questions, leaders inevitably see the need to refocus their orientation in favour of a more external focus.

To give an example, we worked closely with a market-leading B2B company in food services that was losing market share, suffering from margin erosion, and, consequently, declining profitability. As a result, the board directed the CEO and the executive leadership team to undertake a major cost transformation exercise over 2 years. The initial communication of this initiative

Table 6 Guiding Questions

	Incumbent	Y/N	Insurgent	Y/N
1.	Culture is more defined by achieving your budget, selling more stuff, and kicking "own" goals?		Is culture more defined by serving your customers, beating your competition, and creating value for stakeholders?	
2.	Is your strategy process more budget-driven, i.e., driven by your own internal expectations (and numbers)?		Is your strategy process more market-driven, i.e., driven by finding and capturing opportunities in the market?	
3.	Is your strategy process driven more by your leadership team locked in a boardroom working around a conference room table?		Are external stakeholders, including customers (not including consultants), involved in your strategy process?	
4.	Are front-line decisions driven by policies and escalations designed primarily to benefit the company?		Are front-line staff empowered to make decisions on behalf of the customer, for the benefit of the customer?	
5.	Is your leadership incentive programme mostly driven by revenue and EBIT (profit) performance?		Does your leadership incentive programme have material incentives (both carrot and stick) for relative performance in the market and stakeholder value creation (e.g., market share improvement, NPS, customer satisfaction, etc.)?	
6.	Is your firm defined and constrained by the industry definition in which it operates currently?		Does your firm look outside of traditional industry boundaries for new ways to compete?	
7.	Is your firm playing defence, i.e., protecting your existing position and prioritising Y-axis opportunities?		Is your firm playing offence, i.e., aggressively seeking new X-axis opportunities?	
8.	Are firm processes viewed primarily in terms of operational efficiency for the benefit of the firm?		Are firm processes viewed from the point of view of value added for customers (e.g., enhanced experience)?	

9.	Is the firm looking primarily at short-term industry trends to drive strategy?		Is the firm looking at the convergence of long-term trends shaping the market surrounding and including your industry (i.e., including adjacent ecosystems)?	
10.	Does your firm primarily look to extrapolate existing capabilities to drive growth?		Does your firm primarily look to create new distinctive capabilities that undermine incumbent competition?	

was very internally focused and cost-oriented. The company was upfront and honest to middle management (where the cutting would be deepest) about declining profitability (that said, profits were significant and positive, albeit declining) and the probable need to cut back the workforce to achieve the cost targets set by the board. Within hours of the initial management meetings, confidential messages leaked out to front-line staff and the market. Rumours began circulating about lay-offs and redundancies. Morale plunged almost overnight and there was an almost palpable fear in the business. We convinced the CEO and the board to hold off on the decision to drive the "cost transformation" process for 12 months. It was our strong belief that a process of this size and scope (almost every function was to be impacted by the transformation process) should not be run as an internally focused exercise. For sure, one of the outcomes of the process would be to reduce cost. But the myopic internal cost focus, we argued, would be so detrimental to morale and so disconnected from the market that customers would inevitably suffer as a result leading to diminishing growth. Instead, with the CEO's strong support, we advocated taking a year to get every function in the company focused on the external customer with a laser-like focus on how the firm would serve customers in the future. Almost all functions across the business were engaged in discussions about their customers, how they were changing, how the firm compared to competition, etc. Surveys were conducted to ask customers how the company was positioned in their minds relative to the competition and how employees felt that they could better serve their customers and grow the business. At the end of the year, all of the feedback from customers and the business was compiled and translated into a "customer transformation" programme with an explicit goal to change the business model (X-axis) to "solve for" delivering a far more customer-focused business model focused on growth. As such, cost was not framed as a key objective but, rather, the customer (and growth). By the time the transformation programme was initiated, there was broad buy-in for the transformation and full engagement of middle management. The outside-in focus of the transformation had several benefits: 1) refocus of the culture of the business on the customer and competition, 2) refocus management on growth over cost, 3) the majority of the programme objectives and solutions were co-created with customers and management (including, especially, front-line leadership), 4) the business, in spite of taking a full year of work to change the perspective of the company, was still able to meet its timeline and original cost objectives whilst restoring growth to the business. The company emerged from the process on the front foot with new confidence it had not experienced in years and a leaner and more efficient customer-focused business model.

Principle 2: customer proximity

Customer proximity, an extension of the outside-in principle, is discussed extensively above and in previous chapters, so I will not repeat that information here; instead, we will focus again on the how. To become customer-proximate, a firm must commit itself to moving through the five stages described in Chapter 8 and instil a belief that the firm exists to serve the customer first and the shareholder second. The false notion that shareholder value is the only purpose of a public firm must be challenged. A firm is nothing without its customers, fickle though they may be. For a cautious firm, one unwilling to take risks, explore new frontiers, and bring its customers on the journey, disruption is as certain as it is inevitable. Just as a firm cannot save its way to glory, it cannot grow and prosper without customers. Any firm unwilling to push the frontiers with their customers will be displaced, in good time, by those that will.

Principle 3: hyper-mobilisation

The ability of an organisation to deploy its resources ethically, effectively, and efficiently to deliver value to its customers (and be rewarded with growth and value creation) is its highest-order objective. It should therefore also be the highest-order objective of a firm's leadership. Having decided where and how to deploy those resources, they should be deployed without delay. The decision process should neither be unwieldy nor ponderously slow. It is unrealistic to expect that all decisions will come with perfect data, they won't.

Equally, not all investments will pay the same rate of return. The opportunity cost of survival must be calculated in the mix of decision making. Just as Kodak discounted digital imaging because it could not find a way to make it pay similar of returns as film, any firm in an unstable market context must understand the risk of total failure and plan accordingly. Having made a decision to proceed, it must be done at speed using all available resources (note: this applies to pilots as well as full-scale projects).

One example that comes to mind is an oil company I once worked with. I was fascinated by the incredible amount of waste, inefficiency, and political infighting in this business. They had no real competition, so it was inevitable that they looked ever more inward. Yet, when a well head burst at a drill site, the sheer determination of the business to solve that problem was nothing short of astounding. People worked across functions mobilising equipment and people within minutes and across hundreds of miles to solve the problem. Team leaders were empowered to make command decisions on the ground and solve problems as they arose without management interference. Their problem was clear, their functional bias suddenly irrelevant, the teams worked together as if their very lives depended on it. The following week they would be infighting again. Why could they hyper-mobilise one moment and not the next? Impending disruption should drive this same level of commitment to mobilisation even if not certain. Incumbents are notoriously poor at mobilising resources quickly for fear of the consequences of being wrong, ridiculed, and fired. Insurgents don't have this problem. If the big problems are not resolved quickly, they can be 100% certain of their destruction. Thus, hyper-mobilisation is not only necessary but also sufficient.

Boards, in particular, must play a role in helping firms to move much more quickly. They are often part of the problem, being too slow to make decisions, too risk-averse, and lacking time to engage deeply in the issues, especially as context changes. As a result, the board sends a message to management that the organisation must be similarly deliberative and measured. The problem is that this message gets cascaded and amplified at each level of the organisation creating a sort of paralysis where decisions cannot be made effectively. In other words, the balance tips in favour of risk management over action. This applies equally to public, private, and not-for-profit boards. This does not mean that the board should not play a role to help firm's manage risk. It does mean that sometimes the biggest risk is inaction. The most important role the board can play to help management to mobilise is to place pressure on management to execute and to actively help management identify and remove obstacles to execution. Boards must view themselves as a resource to support the firm by helping management to confront the above questions regularly.

Principle 4: marginal economics

In the Caly's case, we saw the failure of Carl and Ally to recognise at what point their business model will collapse should market share and cash flow fall below a certain point. Blockbuster had a similar issue, not understanding that Netflix (and others) need only take a small amount of share to upend their business model. Amazon understands this very well and is willing to accept losses as it drives its business into the heart of incumbent retailers at a loss knowing well that they must race as quickly as possible to take a relatively small amount of share from the incumbents until they reach the tipping point and the incumbent model collapses. This is what we describe as a marginal economics problem. Many incumbent firms have been too slow to respond, instead putting a watching brief on Amazon hoping against hope that Amazon will not disrupt their core business model. Many businesses are unaware of the "tipping point to collapse". Climate change, healthcare, energy, retail, transportation, postal services, and professional services all have significant marginal economics issues to address. For example, in private health insurance in Australia, as costs go up and more consumers opt out of insurance, the costs go up more for the remaining consumers. As the feedback loop accelerates, costs increase and more consumers opt out, accelerating until the business model is rebuilt or collapses. Sensitivity to the marginal impact of key variables driving the business model must be understood along with the above-mentioned feedback loops that may cause a business to reach a fatal tipping point if not addressed in time.

Principle 5: flexible architecture

Having a flexible architecture for a business is an excellent hedge against disruption. In short, a flexible architecture is the degree of flexibility inherent in a firm's business model; in other words, a flexible architecture means that a firm's business model is designed to be adaptive and resilient to change. For example, Caly's business model could be described as having an inflexible architecture because the business had inflexibility built into the business model on the assumption of perpetual context stability. Caly's was unable to adapt to the change in circumstances (see Principle 4) and was, therefore, unable to adjust in time. Firms find inflexibility in vertical integration, in legacy systems, real estate, overextension of their model, etc. For example, McDonald's, with its franchise model, has a tremendous amount of flexibility built into the business model and can, to a degree, flex up or down with the economy. Importantly, McDonald's can use this flexibility to try new things without creating too much downside risk for the company in the short term (though less true of franchisees). Firms need to understand the opportunity cost of inflexibility. In unstable contexts, the question must be asked: "Is it better to be less flexible and slightly more profitable or more flexible, more resilient to change and slightly less profitable?" (the assumption here is that flexibility and profit are indeed a trade-off, this need not be the case).

Here are a few examples of things that drive flexibility:

- The use of contract labour to make labour costs more variable and less fixed
- Outsourcing of non-core or non-distinctive capabilities
- Diversification
- Franchising or licensing of IP or business models
- Leasing vs. purchase of assets
- Vertical integration vs. supply ecosystem
- Alliances and partnerships (see below)

All firms make a trade-off on a certain amount of inflexibility for economic gain. As market stability erodes, the inherent risk of inflexibility increases. The opposite is also true; stable business conditions argue in favour more inflexibility to gather more value. The key is for firms to understand and model the crossover point and have contingencies in place to improve flexibility should context change and enact these contingencies proactively to extend the time before marginal economics reaches a tipping point.

Principle 6: Agility at scale

The ability of a firm to experiment is crucial to success in an unstable environment. Insurgents tend to place emphasis on running small-scale experiments using rapid iteration to reach a confidence point where they can scale their model in the market. For incumbents, it should be no different. The key is to ring-fence experiments from the core business in such a way that the incumbent mindset does not poison or otherwise suffocate the experiments and, often, quarantining the new business from the core once established. The mantra of "fail fast" is often used to describe the iterative mindset, each time learning, adjusting, and improving. McDonald's Australia and Lego demonstrated this capability, using their superior flexibility (in the case of McDonald's) and customer proximity (in the case of LEGO) to drive experiments at the customer frontier. The ability to mobilise resources to scale experiments with the best prospects can become a distinctive capability, providing significant competitive advantage to firms embracing this principle.

I once worked as part of a team on a project for a large national telecommunications firm in the mid-1990s. At that time, digital switching was coming on stream at a rapid pace and then insurgent Cisco was poised to disrupt circuit switching. I recall sitting in a meeting with a group of about a dozen executives of the incumbent telco while my boss at the time shared his (in hindsight quite correct) vision for the future of telecommunications and mobility. After about 16 hours of discussion of how digital switching was going to change the world of telecommunications and disrupt the incumbent's analogue switching business, one executive put up his hand and said, "That's all great, but how are you going to help me sell more analogue switches?" What followed was a realisation that the core business was never going to be able to marshal the resources or political will to change; an experimental division was created, under the direct authority of the chairman, to stand up a digital-switching business focused on enabling enterprise and consumer applications (i.e., how the customer would use the network in the future) from a standing start. The new business was given a mandate and the resources to *compete against the incumbent business* into oblivion if they could. Only one leader was brought over from the incumbent business to the new business. The experiment scaled up from an idea and, factoring in a few false starts, reached more than $1 billion in less than 4 years. The chairman recognised the importance of self-cannibalisation.

Principle 7: ecosystems not castles

Modern firms are less and less monolithic and more and more co-dependent on survival and prosperity than ever before. Alliances between firms and across traditional ecosystems are becoming more common and necessary. Lego-Disney, Apple-Foxconn, and Tesla-Panasonic are a few examples from the players mentioned in this book so far. As the world gets more complex, creating and maintaining all the necessary capabilities to compete becomes exponentially more difficult. In some cases, traditional incumbents are allying with insurgents (if you can't beat them, join them). For example, to offset the threat of SpaceX (see Chapter 12), United Launch Alliance, already a joint venture between rivals Boeing and Lockheed, has teamed up with Blue Origin, Jeff Bezos' rocket firm, to jointly develop the Vulcan rocket system designed to compete with the Starship and Falcon Heavy (Robinson, 2014). Agile firms recognise the limits of their capabilities and are willing and able to leverage best of breed capabilities to accelerate their efforts to scale (Tesla/Panasonic), reach new markets (e.g., Lego/Disney), or leverage capabilities and capacity (Microsoft Azure/Linux). As such, the concept of competition is rapidly changing and the need to scan for opportunities to link ecosystems must be a key part of the incumbent's playbook. Why take the time to develop the capability in-house if it can be adapted for your purposes? For this reason, firms must increasingly develop the "platforms not empires" philosophy and be willing to view their enterprise as a platform onto which new capability can be "plugged-in" or "snapped-on". This requires an open architecture for the firm and an ability to create interfaces across processes (systems, process, organisation) that will allow other firms to easily and efficiently connect. Process discipline is required to make this possible as is a willingness to be transparent about the "sausage factory" inside the firm. Tesla's openness with its code is a great example of a platform view of the business. Not only can partners more easily interface with their technology, the development of a standard based on the Tesla ecosystem becomes more likely as more firms use the technology.

Principle 8: horizontal leadership

In Chapter 12 we described the changing nature of leadership and the importance of embracing horizontal leadership as a means to more sharply focus the firm on critical problems and opportunities. As the nature of work evolves, horizontal leadership will become more mainstream. Anecdotally, the work content of many organisations we work with is approaching 50% of management time working on projects aimed at solving a particular problem.

This is a dramatic change from a decade ago where less than 10% of time was allocated to projects. Of course, this gives accountants a headache trying to work out how best to allocate costs!

These principles, while not exhaustive, can help incumbents create a starting point to the hard work of shifting the curve back upstream in favour of insurgence. If your business finds itself in an increasingly unstable and changing context, it is essential that you make every effort to make the adjustments described in this book to shore up your position against disruption on one hand and discover how to initiate disruption on the other. It is essential that you have a clear answer to the question "how robust is your business model to disruption?" and that you have a clear plan to adapt your model to changing conditions. As we have seen, more often than not, the business model is not considered as a variable but as a fixed quantity for incumbent firms. This mindset must be changed in order to enable your leadership to guide the business through disruptive change. Can an established incumbent operate like a nimble insurgent in unstable markets? We think the answer is yes. Leaders should take heart that almost all of the variables necessary to develop an ethos of insurgence are under their control and can therefore be changed. Don't fall into the incumbent trap; discover and embrace insurgence as a key source of future competitive advantage.

Reference

Robinson, A, 2014, Jeff Bezos' Blue Origin partners with Boeing and Lockheed Martin to reduce dependence on Russian rockets, *Vox Media, LLC*, viewed 22 August 2019, https://theverge.com/2014/9/17/6328961/jeff-bezos-blue-origin-partners-with-united-launch-alliance-for-new-rocket.

Index

Page numbers in **bold** reference tables; Page numbers in *italics* reference figures.